The Fashion Industry

Other Books of Related Interest:

Opposing Viewpoints Series

Advertising

Consumerism

The Culture of Beauty

Current Controversies Series

Consumer Debt

Fair Trade

At Issue Series

Beauty Pagents

Does Outsourcing Harm America?

How Should Obesity Be Treated?

"Congress shall make
no law . . . abridging
the freedom of speech,
or of the press."

First Amendment to the U.S. Constitution

The basic foundation of our democracy is the First Amendment guarantee of freedom of expression. The Opposing Viewpoints Series is dedicated to the concept of this basic freedom and the idea that it is more important to practice it than to enshrine it.

OPPOSING
VIEWPOINTS®
SERIES

The Fashion Industry

Roman Espejo, Book Editor

GREENHAVEN PRESS
A part of Gale, Cengage Learning

GALE
CENGAGE Learning™

Detroit • New York • San Francisco • New Haven, Conn • Waterville, Maine • London

Christine Nasso, *Publisher*
Elizabeth Des Chenes, *Managing Editor*

© 2010 Greenhaven Press, a part of Gale, Cengage Learning.

Gale and Greenhaven Press are registered trademarks used herein under license.

For more information, contact:
Greenhaven Press
27500 Drake Rd.
Farmington Hills, MI 48331-3535
Or you can visit our Internet site at gale.cengage.com

For product information and technology assistance, contact us at

Gale Customer Support, 1-800-877-4253
For permission to use material from this text or product, submit all requests online at
www.cengage.com/permissions

Further permissions questions can be emailed to permissionrequest@cengage.com

Articles in Greenhaven Press anthologies are often edited for length to meet page requirements. In addition, original titles of these works are changed to clearly present the main thesis and to explicitly indicate the author's opinion. Every effort is made to ensure that Greenhaven Press accurately reflects the original intent of the authors. Every effort has been made to trace the owners of copyrighted material.

Cover Image copyright Gina Smith, 2009. Used under license from Shutterstock.com.

LIBRARY OF CONGRESS CATALOGING-IN-PUBLICATION DATA

The fashion industry / Roman Espejo, book editor.
    p. cm. -- (Opposing viewpoints)
    Includes bibliographical references and index.
    ISBN 978-0-7377-4512-2 (hardcover) -- ISBN 978-0-7377-4513-9 (pbk.)
    1. 1. Clothing trade--Juvenile literature. 2. 2. Clothing trade--Moral and ethical aspects--Juvenile literature. 3. 3. Fashion merchandising--Juvenile literature. 4. 4. Fashion--Juvenile literature. I. I. Espejo, Roman, 1977-
    HD9940.A2F368 2010
    338.4'774692--dc22
                                                        2009038711

Printed in the United States of America
1 2 3 4 5 6 7 14 13 12 11 10

Contents

Chapter 3: Is the Fashion Industry Appropriately Regulated?

Chapter 4: What Is the Future of the Fashion Industry?

Why Consider
Opposing Viewpoints?

> *"The only way in which a human being can make some approach to knowing the whole of a subject is by hearing what can be said about it by persons of every variety of opinion and studying all modes in which it can be looked at by every character of mind. No wise man ever acquired his wisdom in any mode but this."*
>
> John Stuart Mill

In our media-intensive culture it is not difficult to find differing opinions. Thousands of newspapers and magazines and dozens of radio and television talk shows resound with differing points of view. The difficulty lies in deciding which opinion to agree with and which "experts" seem the most credible. The more inundated we become with differing opinions and claims, the more essential it is to hone critical reading and thinking skills to evaluate these ideas. Opposing Viewpoints books address this problem directly by presenting stimulating debates that can be used to enhance and teach these skills. The varied opinions contained in each book examine many different aspects of a single issue. While examining these conveniently edited opposing views, readers can develop critical thinking skills such as the ability to compare and contrast authors' credibility, facts, argumentation styles, use of persuasive techniques, and other stylistic tools. In short, the Opposing Viewpoints Series is an ideal way to attain the higher-level thinking and reading skills so essential in a culture of diverse and contradictory opinions.

In addition to providing a tool for critical thinking, Opposing Viewpoints books challenge readers to question their own strongly held opinions and assumptions. Most people form their opinions on the basis of upbringing, peer pressure, and personal, cultural, or professional bias. By reading carefully balanced opposing views, readers must directly confront new ideas as well as the opinions of those with whom they disagree. This is not to simplistically argue that everyone who reads opposing views will—or should—change his or her opinion. Instead, the series enhances readers' understanding of their own views by encouraging confrontation with opposing ideas. Careful examination of others' views can lead to the readers' understanding of the logical inconsistencies in their own opinions, perspective on why they hold an opinion, and the consideration of the possibility that their opinion requires further evaluation.

Evaluating Other Opinions

To ensure that this type of examination occurs, Opposing Viewpoints books present all types of opinions. Prominent spokespeople on different sides of each issue as well as well-known professionals from many disciplines challenge the reader. An additional goal of the series is to provide a forum for other, less known, or even unpopular viewpoints. The opinion of an ordinary person who has had to make the decision to cut off life support from a terminally ill relative, for example, may be just as valuable and provide just as much insight as a medical ethicist's professional opinion. The editors have two additional purposes in including these less known views. One, the editors encourage readers to respect others' opinions—even when not enhanced by professional credibility. It is only by reading or listening to and objectively evaluating others' ideas that one can determine whether they are worthy of consideration. Two, the inclusion of such viewpoints encourages the important critical thinking skill of objectively evaluating an author's credentials and bias. This evaluation will illuminate an author's reasons for taking a particular stance on an issue and will aid in readers' evaluation of the author's ideas.

It is our hope that these books will give readers a deeper understanding of the issues debated and an appreciation of the complexity of even seemingly simple issues when good and honest people disagree. This awareness is particularly important in a democratic society such as ours in which people enter into public debate to determine the common good. Those with whom one disagrees should not be regarded as enemies but rather as people whose views deserve careful examination and may shed light on one's own.

Thomas Jefferson once said that "difference of opinion leads to inquiry, and inquiry to truth." Jefferson, a broadly educated man, argued that "if a nation expects to be ignorant and free . . . it expects what never was and never will be." As individuals and as a nation, it is imperative that we consider the opinions of others and examine them with skill and discernment. The Opposing Viewpoints Series is intended to help readers achieve this goal.

David L. Bender and Bruno Leone,
Founders

Introduction

"Although the fur industry does its best to keep the cruelty out of sight, suffering is a common ingredient in all methods of procuring fur, from fur factory farming to trapping."[1]

The Humane Society
of the United States

"By being made into a fur coat, that mink's pelt is raised into something higher, just as a tree made into a violin is raised, or a cow made into a sumptuous steak is raised."[2]

Josie Appleton,
Convenor of the Manifesto Club

Mary-Kate and Ashley Olsen are no strangers to fashion. Evolving from their wholesome image in the public eye, the former child stars are regarded as tastemakers and style icons. Their first upmarket label, the Row, saw the fledgling designers graduate from Wal-Mart—where they previously sold a clothing line geared toward tweens—to exclusive retailers such as Barneys New York and Maxfield. Plus, the twins published a coffee-table book, *Influence*, in which the sisters come face to face with the pioneering minds in fashion that have captivated and motivated them.

The Olsens are also no strangers to animal rights activism. Because they have appeared in assorted minks and stoles at galas and functions and have incorporated such textiles into the Row and their other line, Elizabeth & James, they have become a target for the anti-fur campaign. People for the Ethical Treatment of Animals (PETA) regularly ranks the Olsens on their worst-dressed lists, and visitors to its Web site can clothe a virtual "Hairy Kate and Trashley" in blood-dripping chinchilla, ermine, and skunk. PETA has not dissuaded the pair from wearing fur, but they have convinced other celebrities—Christina Ricci and Paris Hilton, for example—to fake the look instead.

Fur as a controversial fashion statement is a contemporary social issue. Prehistoric evidence shows that ancestral humans wore animal skins to keep warm, and the fur and pelt trade was a major industry from the 1500s to the 1800s, spurring European settlement in North America and interaction with indigenous people. The philosophical debate of animal rights emerged in Europe at the tail end of the twentieth century, leading to the anti-fur movement, as it is known today. This was advanced by grassroots organizations in the 1970s and 1980s, such as the Animal Liberation Front (ALF) and PETA.

PETA and like-minded groups argue that the fur trade is guilty of inhumane practices, whether the animal is trapped in the wild or farmed. For instance, they claim that trappers use devices that maim and prolong the suffering of their prey. The most familiar of these is the steel-jaw trap. Reports suggest that up to 25 percent of animals caught by them bite or snap off their own limbs to escape, while others struggle and languish for hours until bleeding to death. And because they are not closely monitored, animals not meant for fur traps—including dogs, cats, and protected species—may wander into them.

Animals raised for their fur purportedly meet a similarly cruel fate. Farmers are accused of imprisoning minks, raccoons, and other free-roaming creatures in cramped, filthy cages. To keep their fur intact and useable, PETA maintains, "trappers usually strangle, beat, or stomp them to death. Animals on fur farms may be gassed, electrocuted, poisoned with strychnine, or have their necks snapped. These methods are not 100 percent effective and some animals 'wake up' while being skinned."[3] Another problem cited by PETA and other groups is the deceptive labeling of garments trimmed with dog or cat fur from factories abroad as "faux fur." Such garments have made it to the racks of Macy's, Burlington Coat Factory, and other stores in recent years.

But wearing fur, save for banned kinds, is a lifestyle and aesthetic choice not restricted by law. Prominent figures in fashion who use genuine fur in editorials and collections, such as *Vogue* editor Anna Wintour and designer Karl Lagerfeld, steel themselves against their naysayers. Not one to shy away from controversy, Lagerfeld famously stated, "In a meat-eating world, wearing leather for shoes and clothes and even handbags, the discussion of fur is childish."[4] Others have criticized PETA for objectifying women in their racy "I'd Rather Go Naked than Wear Fur" ads, which feature attractive celebrities. Also, defenders of fur contend that animal rights activists have romanticized notions of wildlife. "The reality is," insists columnist Betsy Hart, "that animals in the wild will for the most part suffer tortuous deaths by a) being brutally killed and eaten, or being eaten very much alive, by other animals or b) dying a horrific, slow death—alone—of sickness, injury, or old age."[5] As for fur farms in the United States, ethical standards for raising and euthanizing animals are enforced, by and large, according to the American Veterinary Medical Association (AVMA).

Fur will likely remain a cause célèbre, as it has grown to be a $13.5 billion industry. Similarly, other concerns facing designers, manufacturers, retailers, consumers, and advocates—from the relationship between models and eating disorders to consumption and sustainability—highlight fashion's social, economic, and environmental impacts. *Opposing Viewpoints: The Fashion Industry* addresses these and other topics in the following chapters: "How Does the Fashion Industry Affect Society?" "What Problems Is the Fashion Industry Facing?" "Is the Fashion Industry Appropriately Regulated?" and

"What Is the Future of the Fashion Industry?" The authors' varying opinions and outlooks demonstrate that fashion is not a black and white issue.

Notes

1. www.hsus.org, July 8, 2009.
2. *spiked*, September 28, 2008.
3. July 8, 2009.
4. Stephen Adams, *The Independent*, January 2, 2009.
5. *Jewish World Review*, December 18, 2007.

OPPOSING
VIEWPOINTS®
SERIES

CHAPTER 1

How Does the Fashion Industry Affect Society?

Chapter Preface

In 2008, the Italian edition of *Vogue* made fashion history. Its July issue was the magazine's first to feature only black models. And after selling out in the United States and Britain in three days, it was the first *Vogue* issue to be reprinted to meet demand. Furthermore, former *America's Next Top Model* contestant Toccara Jones starred in a fourteen-page editorial, making her the first black plus-size model to ever grace the pages of the style bible. Franca Sozzani, the magazine's editor in chief, claimed that the concept was inspired by Barack Obama's historic candidacy for American president and the fading visibility of black models. "I was at the shows," she stated, "and of all the (white) models, there was nobody who struck me: not one name, not one face."[1] According to Sozzani, only one stood out—Liya Kebede. The Ethiopian stunner was featured on one of the four covers created for the special *Vogue* issue.

As celebratory as the moment was, it reanimated the discussion of racism in the fashion industry. The conventional, if arguable, wisdom behind the lack of ethnic models on magazine covers and advertising campaigns is that they "don't sell." Steven Meisel, the acclaimed photographer who shot the July 2008 issue of Italian *Vogue*, states, "I have asked my advertising clients so many times, 'Can we use a black girl?' They say no."[2] Nonetheless, the numbers defy such assumptions once again. Advertising sales for Italian *Vogue*'s all-black issue jumped 30 percent, while the issue of American *Vogue* to move the least units that year featured blonde-haired, blue-eyed actress Gwyneth Paltrow on its cover. In the following viewpoints, the authors examine representations of race, size, and beauty in fashion and how they shape society.

Notes

1. Jeff Israely, *TIME*, July 30, 2008.
2. Cathy Horyn, *The New York Times*, June 19, 2008.

> *"As models are embedded within the fashion industry . . . it is hoped that the drive for ever more extreme thinness could be stemmed at the source, resulting in benefits for all of society."*

Images of Thin Fashion Models Play a Role in Eating Disorders

Janet L. Treasure, Elizabeth R. Wack, and Marion E. Roberts

In the following viewpoint, Janet L. Treasure, Elizabeth R. Wack, and Marion E. Roberts claim that the "size zero" culture of the fashion industry contributes to a toxic environment in which eating disorders flourish. The authors suggest that the demand for extreme thinness encourages unhealthy eating behaviors and substance abuse among models, while low weight and food deprivation can cause serious health problems. Beyond the catwalk, fashion's thinning ideal has led to the rise of bingeing and other eating disorders in the general public, the authors state. Treasure is a professor of psychiatry at King's College in London, England. Wack is a clinical psychology doctoral student at the University

Janet L. Treasure, Elizabeth R. Wack, and Marion E. Roberts, "Models as a High-Risk Group: The Health Implications of a Size Zero Culture," *The British Journal of Psychiatry*, vol. 192, 2008, pp. 243–244. Copyright © 2008 Royal College of Psychiatrists. Reproduced by permission.

of Central Florida. Roberts is a research fellow at the Eating Disorders Research Unit at the Institute of Psychiatry at King's College.

As you read, consider the following questions:

1. As stated by Janet L. Treasure, Elizabeth R. Wack, and Marion E. Roberts, how does anorexia nervosa affect the brain?

2. What is "binge priming," according to the authors?

3. In the authors' view, how have eating disorders been addressed in sports?

There has been widespread concern that the fashion industry, by promulgating ever-diminishing extremes of thinness, is creating a 'toxic' environment in which eating disorders flourish. The Academy for Eating Disorders [AED] has written a position statement for the attention of the fashion industry outlining several recommendations to improve both the health of the public and that of models (www.aedweb.org/media/fashion.cfm).

The aim of this editorial is to consider the implications of the fashion industry's expectation of extreme leanness on the models' own health and also to set this into the context of public health. The direct risks for the models are twofold. First, starvation has a general effect upon all organs in the body, including the brain, and the impact may be profound if the deprivation occurs during development. Second, the demand for, and overvaluation of, extreme thinness within a culture of scrutiny and judgement about weight, shape and eating, increases the risk of developing an eating disorder.

The Health Consequences of Low Weight

There are many health consequences of being underweight. We briefly consider the impact on reproduction, bones and the brain.

Leptin decreases as body weight falls. Without adequate levels of leptin, the cascade of hormonal events that controls ovulation and implantation becomes disrupted. Menstruation becomes irregular or absent and fertility is diminished. The Dutch famine in 1944 and the Chinese famine of 1959–1961 were associated with a fall in fertility. In addition, children *in utero* and beyond had an increased risk of metabolic and reproductive problems and mental illness later in life. Poor nutrition stunts bone development (in the growth phase) and reduces bone turnover and repair, leading to osteoporosis (the impact on bones in eating disorders is a clear exemplar of these effects). Even minor disturbance in eating behaviour during adolescence is associated with adverse health outcomes later in life.

In humans, the brain accounts for 20% of an individual's energy expenditure and plays a key role in nutritional homeostasis. The brain itself shrinks in anorexia nervosa and there is uncertainty as to whether this is fully reversible. The response to starvation includes adjustment of metabolic and physiological processes and changes in drive, thoughts, feelings and behaviour. Starved individuals become preoccupied with food. [Researcher A.] Keys et al. described in great detail subjective and objective reactions to a short period of experimental starvation in men.

Binge Priming

Animal models explain how environmental changes might produce eating disorders. For example, if after a period of food restriction animals are intermittently exposed to highly palatable food, they will significantly overeat. This pattern continues when their weight is restored. This tendency to overconsume, or 'binge,' when exposed to palatable foods remains several months after the period of 'binge priming'. Not only do these animals overeat palatable food, but they are also more prone to show addictive behaviours to the more typical substances of misuse, such as alcohol and cocaine. Underpinning these behavioural changes is an imbalance in chemical transmitters in the reward network, for example, dopamine, acetylcholine, endogenous opiates and cannabinoids. The persistent priming of reward circuits by palatable foods resembles the phenomenon of reward sensitisation produced by drug misuse.

Translating into the human situation, we would predict that binge priming caused by irregular dieting and/or extreme food restriction, interspersed with intermittent consumption of snacks and other highly palatable food, might lead to permanent changes in the reward system. Several hypotheses follow from this:

(a) if binge priming occurs in adolescence, when the developing brain is more susceptible to reward, persistent eating problems may follow;

(b) people exposed to binge priming will be more prone to develop substance misuse.

Some empirical evidence supports the first hypothesis in that there are developmental continuities between eating patterns in early life and the later development of eating disorders. For example, people with eating disorders report a higher consumption of high-palatability foods (fast foods and snack foods) and less regular meal times in childhood. Binge eating is persistent, with binge eating disorder present on average for 14 years, and bulimia nervosa for 5.8 years. Abnormal eating behaviours in early adolescence precede substance misuse and alcohol use disorders commonly supersede clinical bulimic disorders, confirming the second hypothesis.

Models and the Risk of Eating Disorders

Eating patterns that an individual may have found to be integral in the maintenance of a particular shape during her modelling career may lead to deleterious health consequences and maladaptive eating behaviours that affect her far beyond the typically rather short years of such a career. Furthermore, binge priming might also explain why models have such a high rate of substance misuse.

In addition to the biological factors described above, social factors contribute to the unhealthy lifestyle common among those pursuing a modelling career. Constant exposure to media images depicting thin women reduces body-related self-esteem. A meta-analysis of data from 25 studies found that this effect was most pronounced in adolescents and in participants who valued thinness. Body-related self-esteem is particularly pertinent in young models as it relates to their career success. Criticism, teasing and bullying focused on food, weight and shape issues increase the risk of developing an eating disorder. Fashion models are frequently judged and evaluated on these domains and critical and hostile comments, under the guise of professional development, will increase the risk of developing eating disorders.

Successful Intervention in Other Domains

Prevention and regulation of toxic environments is not impossible. Progress has been made in sports and dance. High-performance athletes are also at risk of eating disorders especially in those areas in which excess weight is a handicap or where aesthetic factors are judged. Concerted efforts have been made in the UK [United Kingdom] to set forth guidelines for high-performance athletes and their coaches in an attempt to reduce the prevalence of eating disorders, unhealthy weight loss and maintenance practices. The UK sport guidelines are based on practical strategies that consider the demands of the sport and the long-term health consequences often resulting from those demands.

Following this template, similar approaches to standardisation of care and health for fashion models could be introduced. Unfortunately, such initiatives are yet to be embraced

"Thinspiration"

Scouring through magazines, clothing catalogs, newspapers, television and the movies, some eating-disordered women seize upon super-skinny celebrities for "thinspiration," a term used on pro-anorexia Web sites to describe admiration for their role models.

Supporters post pictures of their thinspiration favorites on Internet sites and community discussion boards. Popular thinspiration celebrities include movie star Keira Knightley, tennis star Anna Kournikova, and models Kate Moss and Oxana Pautova. Even those like Mary-Kate Olsen and Victoria "Posh Spice" Beckham, who have publicly admitted to their battles with eating disorders, are held up as templates for success.

Juliette Terzieff,
"Fashion World Says Too Thin Is Too Hazardous,"
Women's eNews, September 24, 2006.

by the fashion industry, as evidenced by the recent [September 2007] inconclusive outcomes from the UK Model Health Inquiry. As models are embedded within the fashion industry, which holds responsibility for the idealisation of emaciation, it is hoped that the drive for ever more extreme thinness could be stemmed at the source, resulting in benefits for all of society.

The Future

The current fashion for extreme thinness among models unnecessarily puts their physical and psychological health in jeopardy. Starvation disrupts growth and reproductive function and can have profound and persistent effects on brain development. These risks are particularly profound in young women who, in a binge-priming environment, may be more prone to develop other addictive behaviours. Along with an increased risk of substance and alcohol use and misuse, the risk of developing an eating disorder will also be increased. The longer-term health implications on models' bone and reproductive health are unknown but evidence suggests the outcomes are not promising. The recent guidelines from the British Fashion Council, proposing not to include children under 16 years of age as models, is a welcome first step. Might this be taken further (e.g. legislation on age limit for competitive gymnastics)?

Beyond the catwalk, there are wider public health implications. The promotion of the thin ideal, in conjunction with the ready access of highly palatable foods, produces a binge-priming environment. This might explain the exponential increase in eating disorders seen in women born in the last half of the 20th century and in part also contributes to the increase in obesity.

Public health initiatives can be integrated to tackle both of these problems. The fashion and beauty industry can play a key role in preventing the development of unhealthy lifestyles in young people. Indeed, Body Talk, a prevention programme focused on self-esteem developed by Dove in partnership with the UK eating disorder charity beat (www.b-eat.co.uk) takes steps to modify the unrealistic 'ideal form' both as displayed in the flesh by fashion models and through the use of digitally enhanced photography. More focus on these issues will decrease unhealthy forms of dieting, dysregulated eating behaviours and body dissatisfaction among young people. Although it may take time to change such an ideal we should not be faint hearted but remember what has similarly been achieved in relationship to cigarette smoking. People are now starting to listen to the abundance of scientific evidence concerning the harm that such images hold not only for those paid to portray it, but for those who pay to emulate it.

| "Anorexia has flourished in many times and places with no mass media and no ideal of thinness."

Images of Thin Fashion Models Do Not Play a Role in Eating Disorders

Fred Schwarz

Fred Schwarz is a deputy managing editor of National Review. *In the following viewpoint, Schwarz disputes the allegation that the "thin-is-beautiful" message perpetuated by the fashion, beauty, and entertainment industries is responsible for eating disorders among women. The author insists that anorexia appears throughout history and cultures and is not a product of a weight-obsessed, media-saturated society. Instead, it is related to different physiological and genetic conditions, Scharwz contends, and the call for fashion designers and the media to embrace "normal" body types assumes that anorexia is a willful choice, not a complex disease.*

As you read, consider the following questions:

1. How does the author counter the argument that anorexia has increased over the last several decades?

2. What examples does the author provide to support his claim that anorexia occurs in different cultures?

3. How does Fred Schwarz respond to the demand for models of all sizes?

What causes anorexia nervosa, the terrible mental illness whose victims (mostly young women) starve themselves, sometimes to death? To many observers, the answer is clear: Hollywood, Madison Avenue, and Seventh Avenue. Film and television actresses are impossibly thin; advertisers hawk an endless profusion of diet products and banish average-looking people from their commercials; the fashion industry recruits tall, scrawny teenagers as its models and tosses them aside if they become too womanly. When girls and young women are constantly bombarded with thin-is-beautiful messages, is it any wonder that some of them overreact?

Christy Greenleaf, assistant professor of kinesiology, health promotion, and recreation at the University of North Texas, doesn't think so. She has written: "Girls and women, in our society, are socialized to value physical appearance and an ultra-thin beauty that rarely occurs naturally and to pursue that ultra-thin physique at any cost. Research demonstrates that poor body image and disordered eating attitudes are associated with internalizing the mediated (i.e., commodified, airbrushed) bodies that dominate the fashion industry." The narrative is a plausible one, and it fits a familiar template: Big business uses mass media to destroy consumers' health by creating harmful desires. Yet there are large parts of it that don't hold up.

Not a Modern Artifact

In the first place, anorexia is not in any way an artifact of our modern, weight-obsessed society. Thomas Hobbes wrote about it in the 1680s. A 1987 study showed that anorexia in the United States increased throughout the 19th century and peaked around 1900, when chorus girls were voluptuous and the boyish flapper look was still two decades away. A similar historical pattern has been found for eating disorders in France. Some interplay of genetic and environmental factors may be at work in these cases, or they may have resulted from the common pattern in medicine of certain diagnoses rising and falling in popularity. But it's clear that none of these outbreaks can be attributed to the late-20th- and early-21st-century emphasis on skinniness.

There are plenty of other examples. The medical historian I.S.L. Loudon has identified chlorosis, the 19th-century "virgin's disease," with anorexia and shown that diagnoses of it reached "epidemic proportions" in Victorian England before disappearing completely between 1900 and 1920. A pair of Dutch historians have traced the practice of severe self-starvation all the way back to the early Christians and described the various explanations that were offered for it over the centuries (holiness, witchcraft, demonic possession, miracles, various nervous or emotional disturbances) before a newly scientific medical profession defined it as an illness in the mid-19th century.

All these statistics must be taken as rough indications only. Eating-disorder rates, like those for most psychiatric illnesses, are notoriously slippery, since the conditions are so hard to pin down. Journalists sometimes say that anorexia rates have been increasing for decades, as Americans' lives have become more media-saturated; one source reports that anorexia in young adult females has tripled over the past 40 years. This is a case of the common phenomenon in which growing awareness of a condition leads to increased diagnosis of it, even

Designers, Not Doctors

[Fashion designer Karl] Lagerfeld suggested the weight furor was centered on the wrong end of the scale.

"There are more fat people in the world than too-skinny ones, and the fat ones have big, big problems. Nobody cares; they are not glamorous," he continued. "We are designers, not doctors who have to care about 'eating disorders.'"

Lagerfeld said his criteria for a model were "the right look, the touch of the moment, a personal style and a memorable face. I have never had other criteria. Age is also unimportant, from 15 to 40 and more. It's all about style and modernity, and not weight. If a new girl, like Kate Moss but 'big,' would show up, she could create a new style, a new look—but that may not happen tomorrow."

WWD, *"Skinny Model Furor:
Not All Fashion's Fault, Say Designers, Editors,"
January 30, 2007.*

when there is no real increase in its prevalence. Researchers who have carefully studied the data conclude that there has been no significant change in the rate of anorexia in America since at least the mid-20th century.

Moreover, while it's tempting to blame America's appearance-obsessed culture for the plight of its self-starving daughters, anorexia is a global phenomenon. A 2001 article reviewed the extensive literature on eating disorders among residents of Europe, Asia, Africa, the Middle East, and Australia. In some regions, the reported rates of anorexia were several times that of the United States (though, as above, such figures must be taken with caution). In a case of political correctness attacking itself, one researcher says those who attribute anorexia to media sexism are being ethnocentric: "The biomedical definition of anorexia nervosa emphasizes fat-phobia.... However, evidence exists that suggests anorexia nervosa can exist without the Western fear of fatness and that this culturally biased view of anorexia nervosa may obscure health care professionals' understanding of a patient's own cultural reasons for self-starvation."

Physical Roots

If it isn't skinny models, what's the cause? In the last dozen years or so, scientists have linked anorexia to many different physiological conditions: high levels of estrogen in the womb; low levels of serotonin in the brain; a genetic mutation; overactivity by dopamine receptors; a general tendency toward anxiety and obsessionality; high age at menarche; elevated amounts of a mysterious peptide called CART; autism (which is underdiagnosed in girls, perhaps because it sometimes manifests itself in the form of eating disorders); premature birth or other birth complications; irregular activity in the insular cortex of the brain; post-traumatic stress disorder; an autoimmune disorder affecting the hypothalamus and pituitary gland; variations in the structure of the anterior ventral striatum (the brain region responsible for emotional responses); and even being born in June (seriously—one theory is that a winter-type disease in the mother at a certain vulnerable point during the pregnancy is responsible). Some of these causes may overlap with one another, but biomedical researchers are virtually unanimous that anorexia has physical roots, though the mechanism remains poorly understood.

Might these physiological factors be what makes one susceptible to anorexia, but cultural images are what sets it off? Walter Kaye, a psychiatry professor at UC [University of California]-San Diego, has suggested such a mechanism: "Less than half of 1 percent of all women develop anorexia nervosa, which indicates to us that societal pressure alone isn't enough to cause someone to develop this disease. Our research has found that genes seem to play a substantial role in determining who is vulnerable to developing an eating disorder. However, the societal pressure isn't irrelevant; it may be the environmental trigger that releases a person's genetic risk."

Maybe, but probably not. As noted above, anorexia has flourished in many times and places with no mass media and no ideal of thinness. Anorexia could be just another manifestation of self-destructiveness, like slashing one's wrists. It could stem from some cause unrelated to body image, such as disgust with the processes of digestion and elimination (as well as menstruation, which often ceases in long-term anorexics). Psychiatrists believe that many anorexic women want to reverse the effects of puberty, such as breasts and hips, and while most of today's film and television sex symbols are indeed slender, they rarely lack for breasts and hips.

A Complicated Condition

Despite the uncertain connection, some observers still think the media need to change their act. Professor Greenleaf has suggested: "A potentially healthier approach is to include [in advertising] a variety of body shapes and sizes (as opposed to idealizing only one physique). Healthy bodies come in all shapes and sizes—and health is what should be valued, which may not fit with the fashion industry's emphasis on ultra-thin beauty."

The suggestion is not outlandish. Many advertisers and fashion magazines have, in fact, tried using "a variety of body shapes and sizes" among their models—once. It makes a decent publicity gimmick, but there's a reason they always go back to slender models: Clothes look better on them. (Also, it usually isn't practical to custom-sew garments for individual models, so clothing samples are made for a standard size 6.) And for some reason, viewers of films and television, male and female, tend to like beautiful actresses rather than healthy ones—not to mention the common observation that "the camera adds ten pounds."

If increasing the labor pool for models and actresses by including heftier ones yielded equally good results, the industries in question would have done it long ago. Why deal with a bunch of stuck-up teenagers if you don't have to? If media and fashion conglomerates really do dictate our image of the ideal female, why don't they manipulate us into going crazy for plumpish housewives instead? And even if it's true that media images make some people weight-conscious, the benefits must easily exceed the costs, since obesity is a much greater problem in America than anorexia.

Nonetheless, some lawmakers are calling for bans on skinny models. Madrid and Milan have prohibited those with a body mass index lower than 18 from their fashion shows. (Body mass index is the weight in kilograms divided by the square of the height in meters. A BMI of 18 is considered the low end of the normal range, but you wouldn't expect models as a group to have "normal" physiques, any more than you would expect it from football players.) Similar bans have been proposed in Quebec, London, New York City, New York State, and France's national assembly. The main goal of these bills, which began to be introduced after several models starved themselves to death, is supposedly to reduce anorexia within the industry, though proponents always invoke the baleful effects that waif-like models have on society as a whole. Yet this assumes that self-starvation is a willful choice that anorexics will abandon if given the proper incentive, when in fact it is a mental illness that for centuries has proven stubbornly impervious to rational arguments.

Anorexia is a dreadful disease, and still poorly understood. If the growing scientific knowledge about it can be pieced together, we may eventually learn to identify, prevent, treat, and possibly cure it. But political activists do not help its sufferers when they oversimplify a complicated condition and blame it on their stock assortment of evil forces in American society.

> *"Fear of the full-figured runs through every cog of the industry once you leave the realm of retailers and brands that are exclusively plus-size."*

The Fashion Industry Ignores Plus-Size Women

Emili Vesilind

The number of full-figured women in the United States is growing, but only a slim minority of labels and retailers cater to their demand for on-trend fashions, writes Emili Vesilind in the following viewpoint. Vesilind claims that because of the fashion industry's "fear of fat," most designers are reluctant to create plus-size collections at the risk of diluting their brands' mystique, and business ventures geared toward these consumers often fall short of developing. Consequently, plus-size shoppers have ceased to look for style in aisles racked with designs for thin women, the author concludes. Vesilind writes for the Los Angeles Times.

As you read, consider the following questions:

1. How does Emili Vesilind describe the average American woman?

2. How does the author describe the merchandise available for plus-size women in most boutiques and department stores?

3. According to the author, what happened after Jaye Hersh began stocking plus-size designer jeans and more one-size-fits-all items?

When it comes to shopping, the average American man has it made. At 189.8 pounds and a size 44 regular jacket, he can wear Abercrombie & Fitch, American Apparel or Armani. Department stores, mall retailers and designer boutiques all cater to his physique—even when it's saddled with love handles, a sagging chest or a moderate paunch. In menswear, shlubby is accommodated.

But the average U.S. woman, who's 162.9 pounds and wears a size 14, is treated like an anomaly by apparel brands and retailers—who seem to assume that no one over size 10 follows fashion's capricious trends.

Fashion-forward boutiques such as Maxfield and Fred Segal rarely stock anything over a size 10, and in designer shops, sizes beyond 6 or 8 are often hidden like contraband in the "back." Department stores typically offer tiny sections with only 20 or so brands that fit sizes 14 and up—compared with the 900-plus brands they carry in their regular women's wear departments.

That leaves style-loving full-figured women with a clutch of plus-size chains including Lane Bryant, Fashion Bug, Avenue and Torrid. Or big-box stores such as Target, Kohl's and Wal-Mart, the No. 1 seller of plus-size apparel in the country—though most of its selection consists of basic, often matronly items. Beyond this, plus-size clothing is largely relegated to the Internet, where customers who already have a complicated relationship with clothes are unable to see, touch or try on merchandise.

It often seems that it's easier to find and buy stylish clothes for Chihuahuas than for roughly half the country's female population.

Americans are getting larger, and 62% of females are already categorized as overweight. But the relationship between the fashion industry and fuller-figure women is at a standoff, marked by suspicion, prejudice and low expectations on both sides. The fear of fat is so ingrained in designers and retailers that even among those who've successfully tapped the market, talking plus-size often feels taboo. The fraught relationship between fashion and plus-size is far from new, but seems particularly confounding in a time when retailers are pulling out all the stops to bring in business. Carrying a range of sizes that includes the average female would seem like a good place to start.

"Plus-size has been a challenge for the industry for decades," said Marshall Cohen, chief industry analyst for the research firm NPD Group. "When I interview plus-size women, there's really nothing [in the market] that the consumer says they like. Because of this, women in this demographic have learned to make fashion not a priority." The longing for style is strong, but the hopes of finding it are low, and shopping is less fun than frustrating.

The message board at figuremagazine.com, the online incarnation of *Figure*, a magazine for full-figured women, reads like a laundry list of ways that brands and retailers aren't connecting with the demographic.

"Are all big girls supposed to dress like Midwestern farm wives?" asks one reader. "We have money—why don't they want to sell to us?"

Another adds, "I don't want any more polyester, hip-hop gear, frumpy jeans and themed capris! I want the designers not to assume that I am a frumpy 55-year-old, middle-management employee. . . . Is anyone listening to us?"

It's a which-came-first scenario, Cohen said. Because plus-size women have been ignored for years, they've stopped actively looking for shopping opportunities. But when retailers bring savvy style to the plus-size game (as Gap Inc. did with its short-lived concept, Forth & Towne, which carried fashion-forward clothing for career women in sizes 2 to 20), they often shutter their efforts before they have a chance to bloom.

"Retailers don't have the patience to allow it to evolve," he added. "This is a market that's been underserved for 50 years. Customers are saying, 'For 50 years, you've ignored me and now you expect me to react to it instantaneously?' No."

Designer Line

It's true that the development phase of a plus-size collection is costly, because fitting bigger bodies is more complicated than simply making smaller sizes larger. When bodies get larger (especially over a size 18), they take on a different proportion—there's generally more girth in the middle—and the ratio between hip and waist changes.

But the payoff for sustaining a successful collection is worth the investment, said Rachel Pally, perhaps the only designer who sells a contemporary collection in trendy boutiques and a plus-size line—Rachel Pally White Label—in department stores. Pally's full-figured collection is one of the top-selling vendors for Nordstrom.

"Fashion-forward plus-size women have no options," she said. "They're so thirsty for the product." Why others don't jump on the bandwagon, she added, is a mystery. "It's like, 'Hello? Don't you guys want to make money?'"

Many retailers aren't even game to discuss "plus." When contacted for this story, nearly every major retailer—including Nordstrom, Macy's, H&M, even Wal-Mart—declined to give interviews on the subject or didn't respond to requests. It's an odd silence, considering how ripe the market is. With hardly any high-end resources at their disposal, full-figured women still spent $18.6 billion on apparel in stores and online from December 2007 to November 2008, according to NPD Group.

That's only around 20% of the $109.7 billion spent in the regular-size ranges, but bricks-and-mortar plus-size retailers comprise far less than 20% of the total women's apparel retail industry—and high-end options in the category are extremely rare, so purchase prices are substantially lower.

At the crux of the inequity, according to some plus-size designers, models and retailers, is prejudice toward women the industry doesn't find particularly glamorous or sexy. Like fifth-grade girls who secretly live in fear of being ostracized from the cool clique, they don't want to be caught talking to the fat girl.

Full-figured supermodel Emme sells her own plus-size collection, me by Emme, on QVC, and will be debuting Emme Style, an online clearinghouse for plus-size fashion resources, this year [2009] under the same name. Top fashion magazine editors and designers, she said, are guilty of perpetuating the idea that full-figured women and fashion don't mix.

"It really does come from very few edicts from a few people," she said. "You have to ask yourself why they are [defending] against this. Seriously, there are issues there."

"A Lot of Resistance"

Fear of the full-figured runs through every cog of the industry once you leave the realm of retailers and brands that are exclusively plus-size. "My sales team was adamantly opposed to me doing a plus-size line," said Pally, because they feared it would cause her signature line to lose cachet.

"There was a lot of resistance, but I did it anyway. I used to say my brand was for everyone, but it really wasn't." She's not concerned, she said, with "the few . . . who are offended that I'm accommodating women who make up the majority of the population."

Retailers Offer Young Plus-Size Women Few Options

The young, plus-size shopper, generally defined as a woman who wears a size 14 or greater, is becoming increasingly important to retailers. . . . Yet many young, plus-size women say they are belittled in stores, relegated to buying online—or ignored, period.

As of this spring, shoppers . . . have two fewer options: H&M and Jennifer Lopez's Sweetface Fashion LLC, brands known for style-conscious yet relatively affordable clothing, are discontinuing their plus-size lines in the United States.

The moves struck some industry watchers as counterintuitive—if only because Americans are becoming heavier. In 2002, 16 percent of teens were considered overweight, more than triple the figure in 1980. The average woman in her twenties weighs almost 29 pounds more than women did in 1960, according to the Centers for Disease Control and Prevention.

Suzanne D'Amato,
"Fashion's Larger Problem: Retailers Offer Young
Plus-Size Women Few Options for a Stylish Wardrobe,"
The Washington Post Online, *May 31, 2005.*

Designers whose bread and butter rests on their ability to create an aura of cool exclusivity (basically, the bulk of designers seen on the runway, save brands with lifestyle extensions, such as Michael Kors and Calvin Klein) worry that sallying into the market will dilute their brand's mystique and, ultimately, their sales. Prada designer Miuccia Prada may have had these concerns in mind when she stated that she would not sell clothes over a size 10.

And it's on these loftiest of perches that the hypocrisy of the fashion industry seems most glaring. Some of the world's most lauded designers and fashion critics are—or have at one time been—too broad in the beam to fit a leg into the designs they create and coo over.

Still, compassion is in short supply. When Chanel designer Karl Lagerfeld, who spent most of his adult life battling a serious weight problem, created a capsule collection for H&M in 2004, the newly svelte designer was incensed that the retailer manufactured the collection in larger sizes. "What I designed was fashion for slender and slim people," he said. And in an interview in the March [2009] issue of *Harper's Bazaar*, he sniffed, "The body has to be impeccable . . . if it's not, buy small sizes and less food." Issues, indeed.

While it was heartening to see that *Vogue*'s influential editor Anna Wintour styled plus-size British chanteuse Adele for this year's Grammy Awards, we probably won't be seeing the singer on the cover of the magazine any time soon. ("Most of the *Vogue* girls are so thin, tremendously thin, because Miss Anna don't like fat people," *Vogue* editor-at-large André Leon Talley told Oprah Winfrey in 2005.)

Whitney Thompson, the only plus-size winner of *America's Next Top Model*, said: "I just want to see a size 6 model once on a runway." A perfectly proportioned 5 foot 10 inches tall who wears a size 10 or 12, depending on the garment, she's the first plus-size model to win Tyra Banks's TV modeling competition, though growing up in Florida, she considered herself to be on the slender side. "I'm not a plus-size person, I'm a plus-size model," noted the 21-year-old. "On the street, I'm skinny. At castings, I'm a cow."

What? No 4s?

But it doesn't take a casting call to make plus-size women feel like cultural lepers. They just have to cruise into any of L.A.'s trendiest boutiques, which create the illusion that this is a town of size 0s and 2s. Fraser Ross, owner of the Kitson boutiques, said he wishes more trendy brands would manufacture 12s and 14s—but he adds that he doesn't have the square footage to carry true plus sizes.

"Stores feel they don't want to give in to women with more flesh," Emme said. "There's this idea of slovenliness and all those stereotypes and myths that have been embraced since the '50s. It's ridiculous."

Certainly, there are enough retailers out there to ensure that plus-size women won't be walking around naked any time soon. But resources for fuller-figured women looking to follow trends (and even dabble in the avant-garde) are close to nil. The perception in the industry, said Cohen and Pally, is that full-figured women have less disposable income, and are less concerned with current styles.

This may or may not be another Catch-22. Did the demographic give up on fashion before fashion gave up on the demographic? Or was it the other way around?

Jaye Hersh, owner of the L.A. boutique Intuition on West Pico Boulevard, discovered that the fashion-conscious plus-size customer—who has money to spend—is one of the most underserved markets around when she started stocking designer jeans in sizes 32 to 38, and upping her inventory of one-size-fits-all merchandise.

What started as a slow trickle of customers has ballooned into a voracious new client base. "'Enthusiastic' is an understatement," she said of the reception. The business has helped buoy Hersh's company, while other boutiques in L.A. have shuttered en masse this past year.

Similar tales of success would no doubt blossom should more companies decide to start thinking big.

Emme, who was once called a "fatty" by a photographer who refused to shoot her (she was 5 foot 11 inches tall and a size 10), said responsiveness to the average woman can't come quickly enough. "The market has to change—fashion can't be just for the exclusive few," she said. "We're responsible for ourselves. They're responsible for clothing us."

VIEWPOINT 4

> "It might be over with these thin, thin
> girls. And maybe the real woman will
> come back."

Plus-Size Models Are Becoming More Visible in the Fashion Industry

Elizabeth Bryant

Elizabeth Bryant writes for the San Francisco Chronicle Foreign
Service. *In the following viewpoint, Bryant suggests that changing attitudes in the fashion world hint toward acceptance of a
more full-figured look. For instance, the ban on extremely thin
models in Spain and implementation of health codes in Milan,
Italy, during the last few years are positive signs, she claims.
While it is not likely that high fashion designers will embrace
plus-size women, Bryant notes that requests for healthier-looking
models and rising obesity in European style capitals are prompt-
ing a reexamination of the relationship between weight and
fashion.*

Elizabeth Bryant, "Plus-Size Models Gain New Ground," *San Francisco Chronicle*, October 15, 2006, p. E-1. Copyright © 2006 Hearst Communications Inc., Hearst Newspaper
Division. Reproduced by permission. www.sfgate.com.

As you read, consider the following questions:

1. According to Elizabeth Bryant, how has Johanna Dray's modeling career flourished?

2. Why are attitudes toward size changing in France, as stated by Bryant?

3. What is Wolf Lueck's opinion of extremely thin models?

At 31, Johanna Dray is breathtakingly beautiful, with shoulder-length black hair and big, dark eyes. When she stands up, however, she reveals what has kept her out of most major fashion magazines and catwalks in Europe, including this month's Paris fashion shows: a voluptuous figure clad, one recent evening, in chic black pants.

"The fashion industry is still really snobby," said Dray, who became one of France's first plus-size models a decade ago, and remains among the country's most successful. "There are only a handful of designers who have used big women for their shows. It's still pretty closed."

Whether Europe's top fashion houses will ever embrace the big-is-beautiful look after the controversy now raging over anorexic models is still anybody's guess. Last month [September 2006], Madrid's major fashion show applied weight limits to models for the first time, barring five super thin girls from joining the catwalk. Milan passed codes requiring models to carry medical certificates indicating they are healthy, starting next February [2007].

In London, Britain's Minister for Women Tessa Jowell urged the fashion industry to boycott waiflike models and backed a campaign started by several fashion leaders to overhaul a media-driven image of size zero beauty. And in France, the Health Ministry is debating a series of voluntary measures to regulate the fashion industry, including a charter promoting a more full-figured look.

Fueling European concerns is not only the health of rail-thin models but also fashion's celebration of slenderness that may tilt vulnerable young women toward anorexia.

"A few years ago, people would find this argument exaggerated—anorexia isn't created by the fashion industry," said Dr. Philippe Jeammet, professor of child and adolescent psychiatry at the University of Rene Descartes Paris V, in the French capital. "But anorexics are easily influenced by the images they receive from society."

Still, there is little indication of a revolution in sight. Fashion "cannot be regulated," Didier Grumbach, president of the French Fashion Federation, told the Agence France-Presse [AFP] news agency recently—summing up, observers say, conventional wisdom and the sentiments of many in the industry. If France followed Madrid's efforts to ban super thin models, Grumbach said, "Everybody would laugh."

"I don't think things will change in the foreseeable future," agreed Sylvie Fabregon, head of the Contrebande modeling agency in Paris, which has a plus-size branch. "Remember Twiggy?" she asked, recalling the 1960s supermodel. "People have always liked skinny models."

Scattered Exceptions

There are scattered exceptions. Fashion designer John Galliano has occasionally used large models—including Dray, who appeared in his Paris fashion show last year. But she was shocked by a subsequent spread in *Vogue* magazine of the show—which also featured extremely tall and short models, as well as chunky ones.

"Their theme was something like 'Freak is chic,'" said Dray, sipping Diet Coke at a restaurant across from the Dior fashion house in Paris on a recent evening. "I was really insulted. I don't feel like I'm a freak."

At 5 feet 9 inches, and wearing the equivalent of a size 16—the pear-shaped model declines to say exactly how much

Potential Profit

In the last 20 years, the rate of *obesity* among adolescents age 12–19 has more than tripled, increasing from 5 percent to 17.6 percent, according to a National Health and Nutrition Examination survey. Catering to bigger teens could potentially mean bigger bucks for the fashion industry, which has been adversely affected by the recession.

Lola Ogunnaike,
"Fashion Stretches to Fit Plus-Size Teens,"
CNN.com, April 29, 2009.

she weighs but appears to the casual observer to be somewhere between "generous" and normal—she is certainly not fat by American standards, but perhaps a bit heavy to the ever weight-conscious French.

Indeed, Dray is used to stares from strangers in France—but not for being a "freak." Photographers would follow her as a young fashion student around Paris. Finally, one shooter approached her in the subway and asked if she modeled.

"I told him: 'Look, I'm not skinny,'" she recalled. "He said: 'That's exactly what we're looking for.'"

Her first client was the ready-to-wear brand Giani Forte for plus-size women, which still uses Dray in its catalogs. She has since branched out to model for catalogs in Belgium and Germany, and appeared in several major magazines. An *Elle* magazine special on full-figured women featured Dray wearing nothing but jewels.

"I think the fact that I work as a model, that I appear in magazines, really reassures many women," Dray said. "It sends them the signal they have the right to be themselves."

More recently, she has been solicited by France's news media to talk about haute couture's unstated but widely practiced boycott of large models.

"It's really good that people are saying stop," Dray said of the Madrid and Milan crackdowns. "But when things really start to change is when a magazine like *Vogue* uses a girl like me on its cover."

Progressing Mentalities

Expanding waistlines may help drive the change. Obesity is becoming a fact of life in Europe, as it is in the United States. A survey released last month [September 2006] by France's TNS Sofres polling agency, for example, found that 12.4 percent of French adults were obese—nearly a 10 percent jump since 2003. Obesity is even more prevalent in countries like Britain and Italy.

And the notoriously cigarette-friendly French lost a prop against obesity this month, when the prime minister announced a ban on smoking in schools, offices and public buildings starting in February [2007], with restrictions kicking in at restaurants, dance clubs and some bars in 2008. This may finally be the time when they re-examine their attitudes on weight too—but don't hold your breath.

At Cazak, an elegant plus-size boutique off the Champs-Élysées, store owner Karen Hansen said her mushrooming clientele includes wives of top politicians and businessmen. But so far, she says, only one famous designer—Gianfranco Ferré—carries a ready-to-wear brand for larger-size women.

"They're like ostriches—pretending that the problem doesn't exist so that maybe it will go away," she says of other designers.

But in Germany, model agency owner Wolf Lueck believes mentalities are progressing. "We're seeing healthier-looking models in Germany," he said. "It's a little odd to have these pale, skinny girls—totally flat, with no butts. Unsexy." Still, the full-figured look mostly showcases catalogs and not the haute couture world. But fashion is fashion, Lueck notes, and it likes new trends.

"Who knows?" he mused. "It might be over with these thin, thin girls. And maybe the real woman will come back."

> *"It's almost as if the industry dictates this blond, blue-eyed ideal."*

The Fashion Industry Lacks Ethnic Diversity

Anne Bratskeir

Anne Bratskeir is a fashion writer for Newsday. *In the following viewpoint, Bratskeir maintains that models of color are an exception on runways, where the overwhelming majority is white and often blond. The author states that casting agents, editors, and other insiders are aware of the lack of diversity in fashion shows—save for the token black model—but acknowledge that a designer's or client's aesthetic choices come before obligations to represent race. The marketplace also dictates these choices, Bratskeir claims, and some players in the fashion world are hoping for change.*

As you read, consider the following questions:

1. In Bethann Hardison's opinion, what has happened to the fashion industry?

2. According to the viewpoint, how are modeling agencies responsible for the lack of ethnic models?

Anne Bratskeir, "Diversity May Be Fashion Week's Latest Victim," *Newsday*, vol. 198, January 30, 2008. Copyright © 2008 Newsday Inc. Reproduced by permission. www.newsday.com.

3. How did the Council of Fashion Designers of America (CFDA) respond to the issue of ethnic diversity, as stated by Anne Bratskeir?

"There should be more than one spot for a black model," says Yordanos Teshager, 21, a reed-thin, nearly 6-foot-tall model from Ethiopia who is represented by the prestigious Elite agency. But despite going on 85 cast calls seeking work during Fashion Week last season, she says she often left feeling that "they were going to hire a white girl."

They did. Teshager walked in only 11 of some 200 shows last September [2007], a season in which, overall, women of color were glaringly absent. Of the 101 shows and presentations posted on Style.com, more than a third employed no black models, according to an article in *Women's Wear Daily*.

Models were a homogeneous bunch—overwhelmingly white, bony and often blond. Along with the obvious—and serious—issue of racism, some wondered whether it wasn't all becoming just a little boring. Which is why, when Fashion Week opens tomorrow [January 31, 2008] at [New York City's] Bryant Park, observers won't just be looking at the clothes—they'll also be looking for a serious change in who's wearing them.

"I would hope some of the designers would mix it up this season. Unless you were Eastern European, white, extremely skinny . . . you didn't fit into the shows last season," says Nigel Barker, the photographer and judge on TV's *America's Next Top Model*.

"Some shows had just one black model," Barker says, adding that he found the shows monotonous, visually unexciting and depressing. "Fashion is about fantasy, and everybody's fantasy is not to be 6 feet [tall] and white."

"I think designers will be more mindful," says Jasmine H. Chang, executive fashion editor of *O, the Oprah Magazine*. Chang says the absence of black models last season made her feel "uncomfortable. Here I am seated in an audience with every ethnicity in the world, and I did feel it was wrong."

Efforts from the Inside

If there is a change, it will be in no small part because of the efforts of former model and agent Bethann Hardison, who has organized three panel discussions since September [2007] on the lack of diversity on runways. And it's a problem that's been building, she says. "It's not just a bad year, it's been a bad decade."

Who does she blame for the runway whiteout? "I blame us all—the designers, the agents, myself. . . . But for me it all starts with the fashion designer," Hardison says. "They've gotten very *Stepford Wives*, lost in commerce, very conservative. . . . Where is the glamour? The avant-garde? I'm trying to get designers to stop following the yellow brick road."

Though she particularly advocates for African Americans, Hardison says the problem affects all races and she vehemently objects to the apparent new taboo of looking different. "Forget even a white girl with style and personality. . . . Fashion is going backwards." Bottom line, Hardison says, "The fashion designer no longer relates to the model, and I believe this is where I can raise consciousness and generate a sense of responsibility. It's race-based, and race conscious and that makes it unconsciously racist."

John Mincarelli, a longtime professor of fashion merchandising at the Fashion Institute of Technology in Manhattan, who takes a sociological view of fashion, agrees. "There's a complete lack of personality and that has to come from the designer. It's a dictate. Black models always bring personality to the runway."

Designer Carmen Marc Valvo, who dresses plenty of women of color including Vanessa Williams, Jennifer Hudson and Queen Latifah, says he's well aware of the issue and makes

No Less Clear

The exclusion is rarely subtle. An agent for the modeling firm Marilyn once told *TIME* magazine of receiving requests from fashion clients that boldly specified "Caucasians only."

The message is not always so blatant these days, but it is no less clear. Take for example the case of two young models, one white, one black, both captivating beauties at the start of their careers. Irina Kulikova, a feline 17-year-old Russian, appeared on no fewer than 24 runways in New York last month [September 2007], a success she went on to repeat in Milan with 14 shows, and in Paris with 24 more. Honorine Uwera, a young Canadian of Rwandan heritage, was hired during the New York season for just five runway shows.

Guy Trebay,
"Ignoring Diversity, Runways Fade to White,"
The New York Times, *October 14, 2007.*

it his business to include a variety of ethnicities in his show. "It's almost as if the industry dictates this blond, blue-eyed ideal. We are very cognizant of this and always include women of color. I think it's almost criminal that one-third of the shows were all white."

Blaming the Agencies

But casting agent Jennifer Starr, who is also a judge on Bravo's *Make Me a Supermodel* and is casting for Ralph Lauren, J. Mendel, Alice Temperley and Carlos Miele, believes the problem stems from the modeling agencies.

"It's not the designers' fault ... at least the designers I work for," she says. "Ralph Lauren, especially, is constantly asking me why there aren't more African American models he can put in his show." Starr says the agencies don't seek out African American women of the same level as the white women they take on. She says she would hope that designers would want diversity, but, she adds, "I don't feel anyone should compromise their aesthetic just to be more representational. They should use the girls they love, whether that girl is white, black, Hispanic or Asian."

Likewise, Kate Armenta, the bookings editor at *Vogue* magazine, says, "The black presence has somewhat faded and there seems to be a lack of up-and-coming black women. We see some, but not enough." She adds that other racial groups are underrepresented as well.

Daul Kim, 18, a Korean model also at Elite, has felt the cold shoulder. In Paris last season, she was actually told at a casting that they were only hiring white women. "I think it was so rude," Kim says. Not to worry, though. This season, Kim was named one of the "Top 10 Models to Watch" by *New York Magazine* and is, according to her agent, "surging a bit in popularity."

Not surprisingly, modeling agencies don't want to take the blame for the dearth of diversity. Roman Young, the director of new faces at Elite, says, "We are doing our part. This is a blended office ethnically and culturally. I'm really passionate about the beauty spectrum." Young says that when a client asks for "the girl next door," he responds that "the girl next door to me was Filipino. . . . Can I send a black girl?" Although he says he's fully aware that the client wants a white model, he notes that in the end, "It's my job to sell beauty, not ethnicity."

Getting Behind Change

Calling for an end to all the finger pointing, Ivan Bart, senior vice president of powerhouse agency IMG Models who represents black supermodels like Alek Wek, Liya Kebede and

Naomi Campbell, says this should be "about the industry coming together and recognizing what the consumer wants. There's a diverse group of consumers out in America and we should be listening to them."

He is optimistic that this season's runways will feature more diversity. In fact, he says IMG has a slew of new ethnic talent to help fill the bill.

Ford Models president John Caplan adds, "Our role, and the role of the agent, is to scout for interesting faces of all ethnicities. . . . The responsibility for who is successful comes down to what the marketplace wants." Well in advance of Fashion Week, Ford's superstar Chanel Iman Robinson, who was often the single black face in shows last season, was already reserved for most of the major shows.

For its part, the Council of Fashion Designers of America [CFDA] is taking a hands-off approach to the issue, though it did send members a letter that touched upon it by saying that "fashion can impact how individuals define themselves so it is the responsibility of the industry to take action to celebrate diversity."

Will it? Elite's Young has noticed "more girls of color on the request list this season." And that holds true at Ford, as well. Hardison is hopeful. "If I was dealing with homeland security, I know nothing would change. But I think it's going to make a difference. You got to keep on, keep on, keep on."

*"Today, coolness lives among youth of
color and their beloved hip-hop."*

Ethnic Diversity in the Fashion Industry Is Improving

Ryan Pintado-Vertner

*In the following viewpoint, Ryan Pintado-Vertner writes that the
increasing diversity in the fashion world is a result of the profitability of hip-hop. As Levi Strauss & Company's former marketing agency once said, "Many white teens identify with black culture, which they find powerful and attractive." Images of models
of color, primarily hip-hop artists already popular with youth,
fill billboards, when ten years ago this was unseen. Ryan Pintado-
Vertner argues that youth of color are a demographic that cannot be ignored in order for a company to succeed. Finally, the
fashion industry is realizing that "coolness lives among youth of
color and their beloved hip-hop." However, these companies tend
to make a profit out of hip-hop culture, particularly Latin hip-
hop culture, while they continue to exploit Latin American workers. Ryan Pintado-Vertner is co-director of DataCenter, a national research organization based in Oakland.*

Ryan Pintado-Vertner, "From Sweatshop to Hip-Hop," *Colorlines*, Issue 17, Summer
2002, p. 35. Reproduced by permission.

As you read, consider the following questions:

1. Who does Ryan Pintado-Vertner say were dismissed by fashion insiders as "sociopaths" during the 1980s and early 1990s?

2. What does the author consider the one basic truth about hip-hop?

3. According to Pintado-Vertner, why did it take so long for the fashion industry to catch on to the profitability of hip-hop?

India.Arie is smiling down at you from a Gap billboard. A half-mile later, it is progressive hip-hop crew Black Eyed Peas looking fresh in Levi's Silver Tab jeans. Rewind two years, and it was Mos Def and Talib Kweli, then De La Soul.

Rewind 10 years, and hip-hop was absent in the mainstream fashion industry. The billboards would have featured thin, slightly curved white female models who refused to smile.

Ten years ago, when Gap Inc. and Levi Strauss & Company gazed into the future of their clothing empires, youth of color were an irrelevant demographic. The fashion powerhouses believed that hip-hop was an annoyingly violent fad that would pass through like a bullet. They gambled against hip-hop. And so far, they have lost millions.

Fashion and Hip-Hop

Today their futures look very different. Both companies have become lightning rods for bad news. Gap stock, once flying high and helping its Republican founder Don Fisher buy political clout in San Francisco, was degraded to junk status by Moody's in February after 21 months of non-stop losses. In the same month, CARMA, a media analysis firm, announced that among U.S. retailers, Gap had received the second-worst media coverage in the world, second only to bankrupt Kmart.

Meanwhile, Levi Strauss & Company has been losing profits—and laying off workers—in what seems to be an irreversible downhill slide in U.S. sales. It has recycled executives like tin cans, dumped marketing agencies left and right, gone IPO and then reversed course back to private stockholdings—all in an effort to stop losing money.

When announcing their bad news to investors, both companies focus on business details like profitability per square footage of retail real estate, or they talk generally about the need for more competitive fashion designs, or, like everyone, they blame September 11.

Neither Gap nor Levi's confesses to the deeper irony of their situation. Both companies are suffering from a loss of cool—the fashion industry's equivalent of cardiac arrest. Where did cool go? It shifted to the very people who were dismissed by fashion insiders as "sociopaths" in the 1980s and early 1990s. They are the kids shooting hoops in concrete jungles, the break-dancers taking over high school hallways, the American-born children of exploited garment workers. The kind of people who rarely made it into fashion billboards. Today, coolness lives among youth of color and their beloved hip-hop. And now, if they are to survive the new millennium, Gap and Levi's must take that coolness back.

The difference between this reality and what the companies anticipated is enormous. Levi's predicted a cheaper, globalized workforce, and began closing U.S. factories and relocating those jobs to countries like Costa Rica and China. In the 1980s alone Levi's closed 58 plants, putting 10,400 people out of work and moving about half of its production overseas. Gap did the same thing, subcontracting with 3,600 factories in 50 countries by 2001.

As a result, Gap and Levi's, like others in the industry, are the focus of dozens of anti-sweatshop campaigns internationally, which have revealed terrible labor conditions in the garment factories sewing their clothing. Both companies have been sued by garment workers in Saipan, a U.S. territory in the Pacific. The suit alleges that the factories, sewing clothes for a who's-who of fashion companies, including Tommy Hilfiger, Calvin Klein, Target and the Limited, practiced indentured servitude. Witness, a human rights organization, says that in Saipan, "14 hour shifts, payless paydays and lockdowns are routine."

In 1990, Levi Strauss & Company closed a factory in San Antonio, laid off more than a thousand workers, gave them horrible severance packages, and then moved the jobs to Costa Rica.

Jason Morteo understands all of this. He is a 17-year-old Chicano lyricist, beat junkie, and grafitti writer in San Antonio. On Wednesday nights, he can be found at Bruno's, a local restaurant, battling other mcees in the freestyle competition. ("I would have won first place, except the other dude starting beat-boxing on me.") He has a front row seat for what Levi's and other clothing companies are trying to do with hip-hop and garment workers.

"For me, I find it so ironic that Levi's, of all companies, is going to try to make a profit off of hip-hop culture, on top of that Latin hip-hop culture, when there's so many people here they exploit so much," he says. "And the companies do their best to keep that out of the media."

Defining Cool

To bury this negative publicity, both Gap and Levi's spend hundreds of millions of dollars on marketing, showering us with images of cool. For years, those images, alternately flashy and sexy and subdued, were, above all, white.

The formula seemed unbeatable: white models + brown workers = mega-profits. Gap became the largest clothing company in the world. Levi's held its own, struggling at times, but still flexing its iconic muscle. Youth of color continued to be invisible, except in so far as they worked at garment factories abroad. (Levi's code of conduct allows 15-year-old laborers to work 60 hours per week in its factories.) In its marketing, Gap focused on selling khakis to the predominately white professional class and their children, and Levi's left the power of its name on auto-pilot, selling denim to teenagers in department stores.

Then, after hip-hop awoke in the 1990s, reality slapped them right in the face.

They finally got the hint, and the shift is evident on television commercials and billboards across the country. Since 1997, Gap ads have featured LL Cool J, Missy Elliot, and RUN-D.M.C. Last season, Gap's commercials featured deejaying, one of the least celebrated elements of hip-hop. DJs Shortkut and Rob Swift cut it up with Shannyn Sossamon, an up and coming L.A. deejay. More recently, Lisa "Left Eye" Lopes and Shaggy sang in the "Give A Little" television ads, along with India.Arie and Macy Gray.

Levi's focused its attention on progressive artists. It sponsored a Lauryn Hill concert tour. It promoted Mos Def and Talib Kweli before Mos Def's career sky-rocketed. Most recently it has scooped up Black Eyed Peas.

But, like most of the fashion industry, Gap and Levi's were more than a decade late on hip-hop.

"Within a few years, well before 'Yo! MTV Raps,' it was clear that this was a massive movement that would influence everything from fashion to automobiles to lifestyle," says Irma Zandl of Zandl Group, a New York-based marketing and trend consultant whose clients include Gap. "Hip-hop culture has gradually enveloped mainstream youth culture not only in the suburbs but also throughout the world."

Why the lag? It certainly was not for lack of opportunity. Hip-hop has long been one of the most fashion-conscious cultural phenomena in America. In the 1980s, its most popular artists defined themselves with signature products. RUN-D.M.C wrote a hit song called "My Adidas" that transformed the shoe into a cult classic. To this day, people rock the Adidas that RUN-D.M.C made famous. LL Cool J did the same thing with Kangol hats. The list of fashion breakthroughs stretched on through the years: biker shorts, Daisy Dukes, huge clock necklaces, African medallions, fat gold chains, sportswear.

The brand consciousness reflects one basic truth about hip-hop: it emerged from despair. Black and brown youth, trapped in fire-blown ghettos across the United States, used rap lyrics to imagine an antidote to their desperation. They watched as the so-called free market created two very different worlds. In one, their own, emptiness reigned: empty pockets, empty blocks, empty promises. In the other, every edifice, every healthy child, every manicured lawn was a testament to the euphoric, distracting power of capitalism.

Presented with this dual world, some rap musicians became activists. Others simply proclaimed that the clear antidote to poverty was wealth. These artists came to define popular rap culture. They wore thick gold chains, leather outfits, fur coats and eventually Tommy Hilfiger, Gucci, Donna Karan–symbols of their success. In the rap culture they created, wealth and fame could erase any stigma, even the oldest, most basic manifestation of American racism: the idea that blackness is ugly. Murdered rapper Notorious B.I.G., who grew up poor in Brooklyn, once rapped about himself:

Heart throb, never/

Black and ugly as ever/

However/

I stay COOGI down to the socks

COOGI, a luxury Australian knitwear label, sells clothes for more money than most poor people make in a week. The company, which never capitalized on its hip-hop potential, is now teetering on the financial edge.

Crashing the Party

Still, despite the clear evidence, it took the mostly white fashion world another decade to notice that hip-hop, perhaps more than any other cultural phenomenon in contemporary America, is a gold mine of mind-boggling proportions. Two things seemed to block its vision.

One was racism. Rap triggered virtually every racial stereotype possible in the white imagination. The race-fueled controversy surrounding hip-hop in its first decade was phenomenal. Unable to move beyond this visceral disgust, and still enamored of America's basic whiteness, the fashion industry stayed away.

Its second blindspot was mass marketing. Companies like Levi's and Gap marketed to enormous young audiences—from 10-year-olds to young professionals. To cover such territory, companies would shoot for the most common denominators in their marketing strategies. They chose themes and images that attracted the largest proportion of their audience—middle-income white Americans.

But economists and marketers noticed that the middle was shrinking. Economic policy during the 1970s and 1980s created more wealth and more poverty, while reducing the size of the middle class. Race demographics also shifted dramatically, especially in certain geographic regions, as people of color make up an increased percentage of the total population.

Suddenly, the old marketing strategy—aiming for the all-purpose middle—no longer worked. In 1997 a market research firm called Roper Starch released a report suggesting ways to market to the "Two Americas." The new approach was known as two-tier marketing. Many companies, from banks to fashion labels, created multiple marketing strategies for the same products: one strategy targeted the wealthy, the other targeted the poor. For Gap, this meant adding the high-priced Banana Republic label and the discount Old Navy brand—three versions of essentially the same product.

Once companies learned to divide their enormous markets into smaller pieces, it became easier for them to recognize the value of hip-hop. Marketers learned to use hip-hop strategically, while using other approaches for other niches—often all in the same marketing campaign.

But beyond two-tier marketing strategies, trend-spotters like Zandl Group and Teenage Research Unlimited pointed to the real bottomline with hip-hop and marketing: white kids with "purchasing power" were listening to it. They warned that if apparel companies like Levi's and Gap underestimated the impact of hip-hop on young consumers—not just on youth of color, but all youth—they would "suffer dearly," as Irma Zandl put it. "Even today, as rock reasserts itself, hip hop beats and hip hop flava are dominant."

Tommy Hilfiger listened to the oracles. Tommy, one of the companies trying to settle with the Saipan workers, was among the first mainstream fashion icons to cash in on the hip-hop strategy. Its traditional marketing strategy relied on heavy doses of American patriotism, sharp-jawed white men, and New England atmosphere to compete with companies like Polo and Calvin Klein for the men's apparel market.

But then one day hip-hop headz discovered the brand, and Tommy was suddenly, almost effortlessly, the epitome of cool. Without fully abandoning its traditional marketing approach, the company cultivated its hip-hop audience on the down-low with strategies like giving rappers free shopping sprees—and even clothing a hip-hop Santa ornament for the White House Christmas tree. Snoop Doggy Dogg performed on "Saturday Night Live" in 1994 wearing all Tommy gear, and Tommy sales increased $90 million that year, according to industry estimates. On the strength of hip-hop listeners, the company's sales shot past a billion dollars a year, making it the blockbuster label of the 1990s. Tommy got so phat that it even tried to buy its competitor Calvin Klein—the gangster rapper challenging the preppy white model to a fight.

More Faces of Color on the 2009 Runways

Everyone's been talking about whether this season [fall 2009], designers and casting directors would be putting more faces of color in their runway lineups. Well! We have the facts and we're voting a qualified yes. Let's explore.

There were 116 labels that held shows at the recently ended New York fashion week; that's 3,697 spots in runway and presentation lineups. Of those, 668 were given to models of color—which, at just over 18%, is 6% better than one year ago. (And certainly better than in the fall of 2007, when WWD reported that one-third of the New York shows used no models of color at all.)

Tatiana, the Anonymous Model, "Model Behaviors: How Did New York Fashion Week's 116 Shows Treat Models of Color?"
jezebel.com, February 25, 2009.

Rumor swirled around Tommy's rise to power, as some communities of color were suspicious of the company's real interest in them. For years, urban legend reported various versions of the same story: that Tommy Hilfiger, the man himself, told the press (or, as I heard the rumor years ago, told Oprah Winfrey) that he was disgusted by all these hip-hoppers wearing his clothes, because he was not designing clothes with such people in mind.

Hip-Hop and Fashion Marketing

Regardless of whether the rumor was true, it spoke to the basic irony of hip-hop and fashion marketing. In a white-dominated industry obsessed by coolness, the underdog has become the undisputed champion of cool.

And Gap and Levi's are suffering for it.

Though no one believes they will collapse into bankruptcy like Kmart, many think Gap and Levi's waited too long to join the hip-hop parade. Gap itself refuses to acknowledge that hip-hop has played any role in its current doldrums. Likewise, it denies any strategic reason for using hip hop artists in its marketing, and claims no direct interest in youth of color. Gap spokeswoman Rebeccah Weiss puts it this way:

"We chose DJs Shortkut and Rob Swift, as well as India.Arie, because they are talented, we like their music, and most importantly, they express unique personal style. We cast them along with many other types of musicians in order to reach out to many different audiences."

Levi Strauss & Company, on the other hand, has been more blunt. "Many white teens identify with black culture, which they find powerful and attractive," Marian Salzman, founding director of TBWA Chiat/Day, Levi's former marketing agency, told a journalist in 1996. "A typical gangsta rap listener is a 14-year-old white boy from the suburbs. An in-your-face attitude is a marketing hook that screams authentic."

This was a startling shift for a company that was an icon of white American culture. The century-old denim pants were the blue jean of choice for the Industrial Age and the Wild West. By the 1970s, Levi's had been marketed by James Dean, Marilyn Monroe, Elvis Presley and Bob Dylan.

Basking in all of this white nostalgia, Levi Strauss & Company was looking the wrong way when black and brown youth turned the fashion world on its head. "It has suffered dearly," says Zandl. "Its popularity amongst teen boys has gone from 28 percent in '94 to 4 percent in 2001—a whopping 86 percent decline."

In 1996, Levi's began its hunt for black culture by launching a television advertising campaign featuring young black kids scaring the shit out of Wall Street professionals, asking in the tag line, "Do you fear me?" The controversial campaign flopped, but has been followed by many others, including the most recent Black Eyed Peas billboard.

This trend infuriates Esperanza Garza, an organizer with Fuerza Unida, which works with women and youth affected by Levi's plant closures in San Antonio. But she really hit the roof when she saw Levi's mega-popular Super Bowl commercial this year: a young Latino, wearing Levi's and a tank top, was break-dancing down the street in Mexico City, listening to Spanish-language hip-hop group Control Machete (of Amores Perros fame). The featured break-dancer was 21-year-old Johnny Cervin, a Mexican-American hip-hopper from Los Angeles.

"They are trying to sell to us now. We are the new market. They can't fool us. We know who they are," Garza says. While the company courts black and brown youth, she says, it continues to exploit their parents here and abroad. Levi Strauss is closing its two remaining factories in San Antonio in April and "negotiating contracts that are worse than severance agreements in 1999."

Jason Morteo puts it this way.

"It's disappointing as a hip-hop artist, and as a Latin American, that I know something so wrong is done to my people, but people are starting to go out and buy these clothes," he says. "People are so deceived, they don't know the full truth about what this company has done."

Periodical Bibliography

The following articles have been selected to supplement the diverse views presented in this chapter.

Teri Agins	"Women Fall Head over Heels for Shoe Makers' Arch Designs," *Wall Street Journal*, October 14, 2008.
Josie Appleton	"In Defence of Fur," *spiked*, September 28, 2006.
Jan Frel	"PETA: Whatever It Takes," *Alternet*, October 5, 2005.
Robin Givhan	"Society Is Sold on Whatever Fashion Is Selling," *Washington Post*, February 1, 2009.
Ruth La Ferla	"Big Girls Need Style, Too," *New York Times*, June 29, 2009.
J.J. Martin	"Why Fashion Needs Eccentrics: Wacky Hats, Over-the-Top Embellishment, and Garish Colors—Spirited Style Setters Will Always Keep Us Smiling," *Harper's Bazaar*, July 2007.
Suzy Menkes	"Yves Saint Laurent, the Designer Who Redefined Women's Wear," *International Herald Tribune*, June 2, 2008.
Sylvia Rubin	"Big or Small, Fit Models Just the Right Size," *San Francisco Chronicle*, June 7, 2009.
Hayley Tsukayama	"Less Room for Plus Sizes?" *Star Tribune*, June 22, 2009.
Alice Wylie	"Black Model Jourdan Dunn's Rapid Rise to the Top of Her Profession Has Merely Served to Highlight the Lack of Ethnic Diversity on Catwalks Around the World," *Scotsman*, December 2, 2008.

OPPOSING
VIEWPOINTS®
SERIES

CHAPTER 2

What Problems Is the Fashion Industry Facing?

Chapter Preface

With its revolving-door inventory of cheap and chic separates for women and men, Spanish franchise Zara has accelerated the retail cycle. Its in-house designers and integrated factories, which are based in southern and eastern Europe, are able to interpret the latest trends and turn sketches into price-tagged creations within two weeks—a mere fraction of the time other retailers produce new lines. Zara's production runs are also limited, minimizing profit losses from merchandise that sells poorly and driving up impulse purchases and customer revisits. "They've built up an excitement around snapping up new clothes before they go,"[1] states retail analyst Kris Miller. In fact, Zara superseded the Gap in 2008 as the world's largest clothing chain, pushing the sales of its parent company, Inditex, to over $3 billion in the first quarter that year.

Built for speed and flexibility, Zara has been hailed as "possibly the most innovative and devastating retailer in the world"[2] by Daniel Piette, an executive of LVMH, home to Louis Vuitton, Fendi, and other luxury labels. Others, however, are critical of its business model. Several experts have warned that Zara may find itself outpaced by its own growth. For instance, despite a 10 percent leap in annual sales reported in 2009, Inditex profits remained flat throughout that year. And some critics point out that such fast-fashion styles are being introduced up to eighteen times a year, filling up wardrobes with throwaway clothes. "Consumers are simply buying way more than they actually need, and cheap prices are fanning thoughtless consumption,"[3] maintains Lee Bo-Eun, director of the Korea Women's Environmental Network.

As mega retailers such as Zara continue to turn out low-priced, if not trend-proof, designs, concerns about consumerism, the environment, and labor practices are on the rise. The authors in the following chapter debate these and other concerns facing the fashion industry.

Notes

1. Rachel Tiplady, *BusinessWeek*, April 4, 2006.
2. CNN.com, June 15, 2001.
3. Jane Han, *Korea Times*, April 22, 2009.

> "Fakes are hardly new in the world of
> designer fashion, but the problem lately
> has reached epidemic proportions."

Counterfeiting Is a Serious Problem for Luxury Brands

Vivia Chen

Vivia Chen writes for the magazine American Lawyer. *In the following viewpoint, Chen argues that counterfeiting poses a larger threat to luxury designers than in the past. She alleges that the quality and turnaround of high-end knockoffs manufactured in hotspots such as China and Korea have improved dramatically in recent years, allowing counterfeiters to court the bargain-hunting wealthy and fool discerning customers. In addition, insular fashion houses, which have failed at outsmarting counterfeiters through their own efforts, are reluctant to cooperate with each other, compounding the problem, the author contends.*

As you read, consider the following questions:

1. In the author's view, how do counterfeits threaten high fashion labels?

2. What laws has Italy enacted to fight counterfeiters, as stated by Vivia Chen?

3. According to the author, how do counterfeiters copy watchmakers?

Mario Boselli, scion of a textile empire that dates back to 1586, thinks he's found a way to outsmart the counterfeiters who have plagued the Italian fashion industry. A large, courtly man in his sixties, Boselli sits in his showroom in Milan, surrounded by racks of avant-garde clothes. He explains how his company makes a sophisticated synthetic fabric called Jungle for Gianni Versace. Suddenly, he gets up and returns with a swath of the intricately patterned jersey fabric. "It's difficult to copy," says Boselli. "The printing process is too expensive."

According to Boselli, who also heads Milan-based Camera Nazionale della Moda Italiana, the leading fashion trade group in Italy, designers have been racking their brains to thwart counterfeiters. Some are even starting to imbed products like handbags and blouses with microchips, he notes. Despite their best efforts, however, most haven't been able to outwit the counterfeiters.

Of course, fakes are hardly new in the world of designer fashion, but the problem lately has reached epidemic proportions. The First Global Congress on Combating Counterfeiting reported in 2004 . . . that trade in counterfeiting goods reached $450 billion globally. And in Italy alone, the market for counterfeit products is valued at $6.4 billion, of which 60 percent comes from clothes and other fashion products, according to the Milan-based Italian Institute Against Counterfeit Goods (INDICAM). The group estimates that Italy has lost more than 40,000 jobs in the past decade because of lost sales attributed to counterfeits. According to the Associazione Imprese Italiane Alta Gamma (commonly called Altagamma), a Milan-based association of high-end Italian makers of designer goods, the worldwide production of fakes has jumped 1,700 percent since 1993. So it's clear that Italy has compelling reasons to safeguard its legendary fashion sector, the only industry in which the economically pressed country still has global supremacy.

What's more, the quality of the fakes themselves has changed. They used to be poorly made, and easy to spot. But the newer counterfeit goods are made in modern Asian factories, with astonishing speed and precision. And they're not only found on the streets, but in shops in chic resort areas and near tourist attractions. "Instead of producing 500 bags a week, [Chinese manufacturers] are making 25,000 a week," says Armando Branchini, Altagamma's secretary general. Almost overnight, the market for fake Italian designer goods became global.

Slow to React

There are plenty of reasons why the Italian high fashion industry finds itself overwhelmed. For starters, both the design houses and the Italian authorities have been slow to react to the counterfeiters. For at least a decade, there has been grudging acceptance of fakes in the marketplace: Designers, unthreatened by the poor-quality imitations, regarded them as minor nuisances; and law enforcement agencies had other priorities besides waging war on behalf of makers of luxury goods.

But now, faced with better fakes, the industry and the Italian authorities are taking the fight more seriously, pursuing criminal charges against counterfeit producers, using customs to monitor illegal shipments, and raiding producers and sellers of fake goods. In addition, some designers are trying to find creative ways to make their products more difficult to copy.

However, none of these methods has significantly stemmed the tide of illicit luxury goods. The problem, say some industry experts and lawyers, lies less with the available remedies and more with the structure of the Italian fashion houses; they tend to be secretive, eccentric, and driven by a single personality. To win the war against counterfeiters, the Italian design industry has to be better organized, more unified, and run in a much more businesslike way—in other words, winning the battle convincingly would require a whole revamping of the anachronistic world of Italian high style. In many ways, the organizational shortcomings of the fashion houses serve as a metaphor for the struggling Italian economy as a whole. What was once a strength—the independent, family-based business—has become a liability in an age of meticulously managed global brands.

For example, the design houses almost never band together in pursuing a counterfeiter, even when a container full of fakes is discovered in customs. Companies will instruct their lawyers to proceed only when the quantity of fakes is significant (about 100 pieces), says Flavia Cassara, a lawyer at the Milan law firm Rapisardi, which specializes in intellectual property. While part of the reluctance is logistical—it's rare to find a big cache of fakes of just one designer, because each shipment usually contains an assortment of fake Pradas, Fendis, Guccis, and the like—the psychological barrier is higher. The fashion houses guard their secrets closely, and are loath to expose their weaknesses to rivals. "The only way to fight [the counterfeiter] is for the companies to work together—but they won't," says Cassara. "It's hard to convince them [to act in unison]."

The danger posed by counterfeit goods to the Italian high fashion industry is twofold: They don't just cut into sales; they sabotage the exclusive image and brand of the company. "Counterfeits are a major nightmare," says Giorgio Brandazza, co-director of the master's program in fashion at Milan's Bocconi School of Management, Italy's leading business school. A former chief operating officer of Calvin Klein Asia, Brandazza explains that companies spend millions to create an aura of exclusivity around their luxury products, which becomes difficult if the goods are too easy to purchase: "Part of the mystique for consumers is the difficulty in buying."

Getting Serious

Until three years ago or so [2003], many designers claimed that counterfeits did not really eat into their market, because the copies were inferior and only attracted buyers who couldn't afford the real things. But in recent years, with the advent of digital technology, some copies have become quite good—and costly. "There are different levels of counterfeits," says Stefania Saviolo, the other co-director of Bocconi's fashion program. She cites an example: At Forte dei Marmi, a tony resort on the Tuscan coast, well-done counterfeit handbags are readily available through private, word-of-mouth sales, and even on the streets. These knockoffs, aimed at wealthy consumers, typically sell for $300; the real versions retail for $1,300.

The luxury watch market is particularly hard-hit. The industry estimates that two-thirds of the luxury timepieces sold online and in shops around the world are fakes, says Frederic Lejosne, managing director for Italy of Gucci Watches, a division of Gucci Group N.V. "We could have twice the sales [but for the counterfeit market]," adds Lejosne. The big problem for oft-copied watch brands like Gucci, as well as the prestigious Swiss makes, is that the imitators have become exceptionally good. "I can't even tell the difference at times; they get every detail—right down to the gift box," says Lejosne. The result is that Gucci watch buyers, unlike those who buy Gucci handbags, are sometimes unwittingly buying fakes, and that hits the company directly, explains Lejosne.

After years of lackadaisical enforcement of anticounterfeiting measures, the Italian government is getting somewhat more serious. Until a few years ago, Italian authorities considered counterfeit crimes "secondary," says Francesca Negri, a lawyer with Rapisardi. But there's growing evidence, often cited by industry watchdogs like the Washington, D.C.-based International AntiCounterfeiting Coalition Inc. [IACC] and Interpol, that organized crime and even some terrorist organizations use the counterfeit channel to launder money. As a result, says Negri, prosecutors are now investigating counterfeiters more aggressively.

Moreover, there are also new laws in Italy aimed at curbing counterfeits. In 2003 Italy introduced the "Made in Italy" legislation to ensure that only goods actually made in the country could bear the label. Negri says that the law affords a greater degree of IP [intellectual property] protection. Last year, Italy even enacted laws that fine consumers several times the retail price of the originals for buying illicit designer goods. Though there were some well-publicized incidents of tourists being slapped with hefty fines in Venice and the Riviera when the law was first enacted, the statute, Negri says, is seldom enforced.

Having tough anticounterfeiting laws on the books, yet not enforcing them, is typical of Italy's ambivalent attitude, say critics. "We have good laws in Italy, but they are not always applied," says Branchini of Altagamma.

So far, the most effective tool in stemming counterfeits is enlisting Italian customs officials to monitor incoming shipments—especially those from Asia. (INDICAM estimates that 70 percent of counterfeits sold in Italy come from Asia, with China in the lead, followed by Korea, Thailand, and Taiwan.) Companies, through their lawyers, are establishing direct links to customs officials, says Lorenzo de Martinis, a partner in the Milan office of Baker & McKenzie: "You have to react immediately once you get a call from customs about suspected goods," says de Martinis, who represents Giorgio Armani and the youth brand Guru.

Slave Laborers

The majority of counterfeited goods originate from Asia, mostly from China and Korea. People who make them are slave laborers. In fact, most of them are young children—a startling number of these kids are as young as 6—who are taken away from their homes to work in poor conditions, and for as little as a dollar an hour. The counterfeiting industry makes up to $650 billion a year. That $650 billion is going somewhere, and you can bet it's not feeding the poor kids in China that make these purses.

Justin Ng, "Faking It! How Counterfeiting Affects Fashion," myitthings.com, February 25, 2008. http://myitthings.com.

Still Ahead of the Game

Tracking counterfeit goods and intercepting them at the border is expensive and time-consuming. So some frustrated designers are beginning to tap their own creativity to thwart fakes. They're working on the products themselves, in an effort to make copying the designs more difficult, as Boselli's fabric company does for Versace.

Other designers are using the fickle nature of fashion itself in an attempt to thwart copiers. In the hot young designers segment, in particular, companies are changing designs quickly—giving them a three-month life span—and betting that counterfeiters can't keep up, says Baker & McKenzie's de Martinis. As an example, he cites his client Guru, a hugely successful clothing brand in Europe that's owned by Jam Session Srl, a company based in Parma, in Italy's prosperous Emilia-Romagna province. Though its T-shirts with their distinctive daisy motif put the Guru label on the map, the company doesn't always go after counterfeiters of that design, because the "daisy is already considered old-market," says de Martinis. The essence of fashion, he adds, is "all about change." (Guru declined to comment.)

But what are the odds that fashion and luxury goods companies can outsmart the fake professionals? If what goes on in the luxury watch market is any indication, counterfeiters are still ahead of the game. At the annual watch trade fair at Basel, Switzerland, in the spring, counterfeiters regularly photograph the watches on display and reproduce them, down to the last detail, in less than a week's time, says Gucci's Lejosne: "I guarantee you what's shown at the start of the show will be selling outside of the trade grounds or on the Internet by the end of the fair."

For the moment, at least, Italy seems to be losing the battle with counterfeiters. "You can put serial numbers on your products, put holograms on them, send for the police— but at the end of the day, there's not much you can do," sighs Brandazza. "It's part of the game."

Others in the fashion trenches are not quite as fatalistic about Italy's struggle against the counterfeit trade in the long run. In the next ten years, predicts Gabriel Cuonzo of the Milan law firm Trevisan & Cuonzo, who represents various fashion clients, the fashion houses will finally join together, pooling information and anticounterfeiting efforts.

Maybe. But to get there, the fashion houses will have to adopt a more global outlook. Big egos might be dominating the Italian fashion industry for the moment, but that will inevitably change as the industry matures. "The fashion business in Italy is on the verge of changing from a business model focused on individuals to one with a global approach," says an optimistic Cuonzo. If the counterfeiters in China are running their operations with large factories and 24-hour operations, the days of running a fashion empire on the whims of one individual are probably over. "Fighting counterfeits is a business problem and requires a business approach," says Cuonzo. "Sooner or later, you need to think like a multinational."

> *"For every negative incident in which a fake damages a brand's reputation, there is an equal number of occasions on which it helps protect the genuine brand."*

Counterfeiting May Actually Benefit Luxury Brands

Mark Ritson

Mark Ritson is a marketing consultant and an associate professor of marketing at Melbourne Business School in Australia. In the following viewpoint, Ritson proposes that counterfeiting can actually be a boon to fashion houses and luxury labels. For instance, he asserts that the sales of knockoffs increase brand awareness and do not cut into the authentic labels' profits because these consumers would not buy the real thing. Also, Ritson declares that the presence of counterfeits can help a company gauge the demand of its products and the health of its brand.

As you read, consider the following questions:

1. According to Mark Ritson, how is the counterfeit buyer's profile changing?

Mark Ritson, "Fakes Can Genuinely Aid Luxury Brands," *Marketing*, July 25, 2007, p. 21. Copyright © 2007 Haymarket Business Publications Ltd. Reproduced by permission.

2. How does buying a fake benefit a consumer, in Ritson's opinion?

3. How can knockoffs increase sales of the genuine article, in the author's view?

I used to work for the chief executive of a European luxury brand. He once told me about a flight he had taken from Paris to New York—first class, of course! He sat next to an elegant woman of a certain age, who, an hour into the flight, took out her handbag. To his immense pleasure, the chief executive recognised one of his brand's latest designs.

However, his bonhomie faded as he surveyed the handbag from across the aisle. Thirty years of *savoir faire* meant it took him just seconds to realise the bag was a fake. Shaking with anger, he spent the next six hours restraining himself and self-medicating on Cognac. Eventually, he could hold back no more. Leaning across, he whispered to the woman, just loud enough for the rest of the cabin to hear, 'If you can afford to travel first class, you can afford the real thing!'

If the latest report on counterfeit luxury goods by law firm Davenport Lyons is to be believed, my old boss is in for many more difficult flights this year. It seems the prevalence and popularity of fake luxury products continues to grow. Two-thirds of respondents were happy to own fake items. Equally concerning was the changing profile of consumers for fake luxury goods; 20% of the 3m [million] Britons who bought these goods had household incomes in excess of £50,000 a year.

The luxury goods market is tipped to grow to £1 trillion in global sales by 2010. With the top luxury brands enjoying operating margins of 60%–70%, it's not hard to see why many marketers view counterfeit products as the biggest threat to these brands.

Most Faked Brands

Burberry

Gucci

Louis Vuitton

BBC News,
"Fake Goods on Rise to Meet Demand,"
www.bbc.co.uk, April 28, 2006.

Flawed Assumptions

In reality, they are no such thing. The first flawed assumption is that a consumer who buys a fake would have otherwise purchased the genuine article—this is hogwash. A woman does not buy a Hermés Birkin bag for £10,000 because she needs a handbag. She wants the brand and for all the utilitarian verisimilitude of a £200 copy from Shanghai, this is something even the best fakes cannot offer.

It's true that millions of fake luxury handbags are sold each year. But very few of them, if any, cannibalise the sales of the real thing. Davenport Lyons reports that in 2006 only 20% of purchasers of fake brands would have bought the genuine article. I suspect even this figure is an exaggeration.

The second flawed argument against fakes is that they harm the brand equity of the luxury brand. Perhaps, but I would argue that for every negative incident in which a fake damages a brand's reputation, there is an equal number of occasions on which it helps protect the genuine brand.

Let's say you are walking down Bond Street and a young man of apparently meagre income and untidy countenance barges past you with a Gucci bag (the same one you own) slung over his shoulder. You curse him under your breath, but just before you reappraise the great house of Gucci and its fine clientele, you pause and sneer, 'Must be fake'. It is probably not, but sometimes it helps to have genuine brands mistaken for forgeries when brand equity is at stake.

Indeed, counterfeit products may be good for luxury brands. Because they are usually manufactured by lean, market-driven entrepreneurs, they are often the first signal of a luxury brand's renaissance (when copies appear) or of the final nail in the coffin (when they don't). As a result, more than one great luxury house uses counterfeit sales to predict demand for its own brand and gauge its overall health.

Fakes are also often the first place where consumers develop an awareness and aspiration for genuine luxury. After all, Davenport Lyons found a third of consumers for fake luxury said they would be more likely to buy the real thing in the future as a result.

"Fast fashion, with its throwaway mentality, encourages a feeling that everything is expendable."

Fast Fashion Is a Problem

Marilyn Gardner

In the following viewpoint, Marilyn Gardner contends that the accelerated turnaround of inexpensive seasonal styles and of-the-minute trends is helping to create a disposable culture. Also known as "fast fashion," these designs are quickly outdated, which encourage shoppers to pursue the latest fads and fill their closets with clothes they will never wear, she continues. In fact, she alleges that fast fashion is part of the larger problem of modern-day consumerism, wherein products are bought, used, cast off, and replaced with each new generation, crowding homes with clutter and landfills with functional goods. Gardner is a writer for The Christian Science Monitor.

As you read, consider the following questions:

1. Which retailers sell fast fashion, according to Marilyn Gardner?

2. How did "investment dressing" affect consumers, in Gardner's opinion?

3. What does a 19th-century home say about the people who lived in that era, in the author's view?

According to the thermometer and the calendar, it's still summer. But step into any clothing store in New England and the season quickly changes.

Mannequins are sheathed in black and gray, and racks groan under the weight of heavy wools. Just to be sure customers get the intended message—it's winter already—the air conditioning is cranked up to high, sending arctic blasts through the store and making shoppers in shorts and sundresses shiver.

Baby, it's cold inside.

This kind of instant seasonal change has long been a staple of fashion merchandisers, with next season's clothes arriving earlier and earlier every year. Swimsuits and sweaters vie for retailers' space in July.

But to maximize both our confusion and our spending power, in recent years Seventh Avenue marketers have added another element: instant style changes. Stores such as Topshop, H&M, and Zara provide a constant rotation of reasonably priced merchandise. The prevailing philosophy is: Here today, gone tomorrow. So fast is the turnaround that styles may be Out before many of us ever realized they were In. Even high-end designers are playing the game.

Fashion Backward?

Call it fast fashion, and consider it either exciting or puzzling, depending on your perspective.

For customers who like to keep up with the latest trends—the shoppers the industry approvingly labels "fashion forward"—this constant turnover produces heady excitement.

Ethical Fashion

[W]hat exactly is ethical fashion? Well, there are any number of different ways in which a garment can be produced ethically (or at least more ethically)—from paying fair wages, using sustainable fabrics and cutting down the distance they must travel, to donating a portion of proceeds to charity or simply making sure the business carefully monitors and limits its environmental impact.

Kate Carter,
"Why Fast Fashion Is so Last Season,"
Guardian, *July 23, 2008.*

But what does that make those of us who prefer more stability and predictability in our closets? Are we "fashion backward"?

Men in particular are begging for mercy, pleading with manufacturers to bring back their favorite styles, according to *The Wall Street Journal.* Fast fashion is producing burnout.

As an antidote, a new line of clothes called Slowear, based in Italy, promises to keep its styles always available. Down with instant obsolescence. Up with staying power.

Yet even classic clothes have their traps. In the 1980s and '90s, the clever phrase "investment dressing" suggested that certain styles would last a long time. It also presumably made women feel less guilty about spending megabucks for a designer jacket or a suit. Even then, there were always new collections of investment dressing clothes to deplete a shopper's bank account the next season. It wasn't fast fashion, but it was just as seductive an idea.

Beyond the endless flow of money these constant purchases require—"Charge it, please"—fast fashion, with its throwaway mentality, encourages a feeling that everything is expendable. It can foster a sense of impermanence, even restlessness, as a shopper goes in pursuit of the hottest new style. It can also require space—lots of it.

Several years ago, I went through a house in Wisconsin that had been built around 1890. Inside and out, the white structure with its hilltop setting and wraparound porch, had a certain grandeur. But it lacked something absolutely essential today: storage space for clothes. None of the bedrooms had a single closet. Residents hung their clothes in wooden wardrobes and armoires, often only four feet wide. That says everything about the modest amount of clothing early occupants owned. A 21st-century visitor could only wonder: How did they ever manage?

Today, to accommodate mountains of clothes, Americans build houses with ever-bigger walk-in closets, some the size of a room. Shoppers make frequent trips to stores specializing in storage containers to stock up on stackable units to hold sweaters and shoes. And still we have too little space for the quickly outdated clothes we think we might still wear "someday."

Instant Obsolescence

Instant obsolescence isn't just a sartorial challenge. Everchanging electronic devices also help to create a disposable culture. As part of manufacturers' planned obsolescence, consumers constantly receive subtle, insistent messages. The voice of temptation whispers: Your cell phone doesn't have a camera, a video recorder, a flashlight, a calculator, and a GPS. How outdated. Time to get a new one. And you don't yet own a flat-screen TV or the very latest digital camera? What are you waiting for?

With each new generation of electronic gadgets—ever smaller, faster, more powerful—we congratulate ourselves on our progress. But as our closets and houses fill with an accumulation of castoff possessions, sartorial and technological, progress can create its own forms of enslavement. No wonder there's a growing audience for a new magazine called *Organize*. And no wonder publishers keep churning out books with titles such as *Put Your House on a Diet.* Our cluttered closets, attics, and basements attest to our affluence and our easy-come, easy-go approach to possessions.

"Staying power" has its uses. As landfills bulge with unwanted but often still-functional possessions, our throwaway culture could heed a reminder: "Fast" has its appeal and its purpose. But slower and longer-lasting still have their place.

> *"Over a lifetime, a polyester blouse uses less energy than a cotton T-shirt."*

Fast Fashion May Have Benefits

Elisabeth Rosenthal

In the following viewpoint, Elisabeth Rosenthal declares that fast fashion—cheap, trendy, disposable clothing—has its environmental advantages. Even though producing a fabric such as organic cotton is green-friendly, Rosenthal suggests that caring for fast fashion's synthetics consumes less energy and water. Furthermore, she says that other possible options, such as leasing high-end pieces and garment-recycling programs, have yet to catch on. The ultimate solution is to buy less and own less clothing, the author concludes. Based in Rome, Italy, Rosenthal is a health and environment correspondent for the International Herald Tribune

As you read, consider the following questions:

1. Why are teenagers especially attracted to fast fashion, in the author's view?

2. In Elisabeth Rosenthal's opinion, what do manufacturers and consumers fail to understand about fabrics?

3. How can cotton be changed so that maintaining it uses less energy, as stated by Rosenthal?

Josephine Copeland and her 20-year-old daughter, Jo Jo, visited Primark at the Peacocks Centre mall here [Woking, England], in the London suburbs, to buy presents for friends, but ended up loaded with clothes for themselves: boots, a cardigan, a festive blouse, and a long, silver coat with faux fur trim, which cost £12 but looks like a million bucks. "If it falls apart, you just toss it away!" said Jo Jo, proudly wearing her purchase.

Environmentally, that is more and more of a problem.

With rainbow piles of sweaters and T-shirts that often cost less than a sandwich, stores like Primark are leaders in the quick-growing "fast fashion" industry, selling cheap garments that can be used and discarded without a second thought. Consumers, especially teenagers, love the concept, pioneered also by stores like H&M internationally and by Old Navy and Target in the United States, since it allows them to shift styles with speed on a low budget.

A Seeming Oxymoron

But clothes—and fast clothes in particular—are a large and worsening source of the carbon emissions that contribute to global warming, because of how they are both produced and cared for, concludes a new report from researchers at Cambridge University titled *Well Dressed?*

The global textile industry must become eco-conscious, the report concludes. It explores how to develop a more "sustainable clothing" industry—a seeming oxymoron in a world where fashions change every few months.

"Hmmm," said Sally Neild, 44, dressed in casual chic, in jeans and boots, as she pondered such alien concepts, shopping bags in hand. "People now think a lot about green travel and green food. But I think we are a long way from there in terms of clothes. People are mad about those stores."

It is hard to imagine how customers who rush after trends, or the stores that serve them, will respond to the report's suggestions: that people lease clothes and return them at the end of a month or a season, so the garments can be lent again to someone else—like library books—and that they buy more expensive and durable clothing that can be worn for years.

In terms of care, the report highlights the benefits of synthetic fabrics that require less hot water to wash and less ironing. It suggests that consumers air-dry clothes and throw away their tumble dryers, which require huge amounts of energy.

A Trend That Won't Go Away

But some big retailers are starting to explore their options. "Our research shows that customers are getting very concerned about environmental issues, and we don't want to get caught between the eyes," said Mike Barry, head of corporate social responsibility at Marks & Spencer, one of Britain's largest retailers, which helped pay for the Cambridge study. "It's a trend that we know won't go away after a season, like a poncho."

Customers "will ask, 'What are you doing?'" Mr. Barry said, noting that 70 percent of Britons shop at his chain. "So we're doing a lot of thinking about what a sustainable clothing industry could look like in five years."

Consumers spend more than $1 trillion a year on clothing and textiles, an estimated one-third of that in Western Europe, another third in North America, and about a quarter in Asia. In many places, cheap, readily disposable clothes have displaced hand-me-downs as the mainstay of dressing.

"My mother had the same wardrobe her entire life," Ms. Neild said. "For my daughter, styles change every six months and you need to keep up."

As a result, women's clothing sales in Britain rose by 21 percent between 2001 and 2005 alone to about £24 billion ($47.6 billion), spurred by lower prices, according to the Cambridge report.

And while many people have grown accustomed to recycling cans, bottles and newspapers, used clothes are generally thrown away. "In a wealthy society, clothing and textiles are bought as much for fashion as for function," the report says, and that means that clothes are replaced "before the end of their natural life."

Dr. Julian Allwood, who led a team of environmental researchers in conducting the report, noted in an interview that it is now easier for British consumers to toss unwanted clothes than to take them to a recycling center, and easier to throw clothes into the hamper for a quick machine wash and dry than to sponge off stains.

He hopes his report will educate shoppers about the costs to the environment, so that they change their behavior.

Changing Consumer Priorities

There are many examples of how changing consumer priorities have forced even the most staid retailers to alter the way they do business.

Last year [2006] Marks & Spencer—Britain's mainstay for products like underwear and shortbread—decided to go organic in its food business; it now sells only fair-trade coffee and teas, for example. Many executives regarded the shift as a foolish and risky decision, but the store found that sales jumped 12 percent. The store learned a lesson that executives think will apply to clothes.

"Morally, we know more sustainable clothing is the right thing to do, but we are more and more convinced that commercially it is the right thing as well," Mr. Barry said. In fact, marketing the "green" value of clothing, even if costs a bit more, may provide an advantage over competitors.

Surviving on Fast Fashion

Developing countries like Bangladesh depend on the fast fashion business model to survive. In fact, nearly 80% of Bangladesh's foreign earnings are derived from the garment industry. Although it could be said that companies take advantage of cheap labor and production costs in countries like Bangladesh, it should also be said that the citizens of Bangladesh benefit from fast fashion by having stable employment through the creation of jobs in the industry.

"Fast Fashion Is Not a Trend,"
December 19, 2008.
www.sydneylovesfashion.com

Part of the problem is that neither manufacturers nor customers understand much about how and when clothing purchases degrade the environment, since these can occur anywhere from the harvest of cotton or the manufacture of synthetic fibers to how—and how often—the garment must be washed.

"We've got fantastic standards when it comes to food, but it is all brand-new when it comes to clothes," Mr. Barry admitted. "We have a lot to learn."

In their efforts to buy green, customers tend to focus on packaging and chemicals, issues that do not factor in with clothing. Likewise, they purchase "natural" fibers like cotton, believing they are good for the environment.

Cotton Versus Synthetic

But that is not always the case: While so-called organic cotton is exemplary in the way it avoids pesticides, cotton garments squander energy because they must be washed frequently at high temperatures, and generally require tumble-drying and ironing. Sixty percent of the carbon emissions generated by a simple cotton T-shirt comes from the 25 washes and machine dryings it will require, the Cambridge study found.

A polyester blouse, by contrast, takes more energy to make, since synthetic fabric comes from materials like wood and oil. But upkeep is far more fuel-efficient, since polyester cleans more easily and dries faster.

Over a lifetime, a polyester blouse uses less energy than a cotton T-shirt.

One way to change the balance would be to develop technology to treat cotton so that it did not absorb odors so readily.

Also, Dr. Allwood said that "reducing washing temperature has a huge impact," speaking of a significant drop from about 122 Fahrenheit to 105. Even better, he said, would be to drop washing temperature below normal body temperatures, but that would require changes in washing machines and detergents.

The report suggests that retailers could begin to lease clothes for a season (just as wedding stores rent tuxedos) or buy back old clothes from customers at a discount, for recycling.

Fashionable or Sustainable

But experiments along these lines have faltered. A decade ago, Hanna Andersson, an eco-conscious American clothing company, tried offering mail-order customers 20 percent credit toward new purchases if they sent back their used garments. This "hannadowns" program was canceled after two years.

People hope "we'll find new sources of energy, so we won't really have to change much," Dr. Allwood said. "But that is extremely unlikely."

To cut back the use of carbons and make fashion truly sustainable, shoppers will have "to own less, to have less stuff," Dr. Allwood said. "And that is a very hard sell."

And so Marks & Spencer is thinking about whether its customers will be willing to change their buying habits, to pay more for less-fashionable but "sustainable" garments. After all, consumers have shown a willingness to pay more for clothes not made in sweatshops, and some are unwilling to buy diamonds because of forced labor in African mines.

On a recent day outside Marks & Spencer on Guildford High Street, where everyone was loaded with shopping bags, Audrey Mammana, who is 45, said she was not "a throw-away person" and would be happy to lease high-end clothing for a season. She would also be willing to repair old clothes to extend their use, although fewer shops perform this task.

But, she added: "If you cut out tumble-drying, I think you'd lose me. I couldn't do without that."

Correction: March 1, 2007

A headline and article on Jan. 25 about the environmental impact of consumers' clothing-buying habits referred incorrectly to a test by Cambridge University researchers that compared the energy required to make and clean an organic cotton T-shirt to that required for a synthetic blouse. The blouse was made of rayon, which is derived from plants; it was not polyester, which is made from polymers. A reader pointed out the error in an e-mail message received on Jan. 26. This correction was delayed because editors did not follow through on the complaint.

> *"In New York and Bangladesh, in Los Angeles and Managua, hearts starve for the finer things in life as we slaves to fashion reap the product of those enslaved to fashion."*

Poor Working Conditions in Factories Are a Serious Problem in the Fashion Industry

Robert J.S. Ross

Robert J.S. Ross is a sociology professor at Clark University in Worcester, Massachusetts, and author of Slaves to Fashion: Poverty and Abuse in the New Sweatshops. *In the following viewpoint excerpted from* Slaves to Fashion, *Ross argues that garment workers across the globe and in America toil in unacceptable conditions to feed the appetite for ever-changing fashions. He maintains that many of them are forced to work in stifling, filthy quarters and at a harried pace for long hours, frequently forfeiting overtime pay, time off, and chances for a better life. Some economists claim that garment workers are better off than prostitutes and impoverished farmers, yet Ross states that each inevitably returns to her village, her livelihood spent before middle age.*

As you read, consider the following questions:

1. How does Robert J.S. Ross describe the work of a sewing machine operator?

2. In the author's view, how has the garment industry changed since the 20th century?

3. How much do sewing machine operators typically work in Chinese export factories, according to Ross?

It is the afternoon of Passover in 1998. Our home is busy with preparations as the feast that celebrates the liberation of Hebrew slaves is nearing readiness. Our guests have not yet arrived, and I am listening to a tape that I plan to play as people arrive. It is a recording of Judy Collins singing a poem—written in 1911 to celebrate women workers on strike—"Bread and Roses." I want to play this song for our guests because for me it knits the pieces together—the ancient festival of liberation; my father's work as a cutter in the garment industry and his mother's and father's work there too; and my work and mission since 1995 on the new sweatshops in the apparel industry.

Dressed and ready, the festive table set, the house warm and aromatic with traditional foods, I find myself focused on the tape player, playing the song over and over again, trying to memorize it. But why am I doing that, now of all times? I can't sing and won't venture to try for our friends and relatives. Over and again the tape plays, and my lips move with the words as Judy Collins's brilliant soprano brims my eyes. And then a phrase leaps at, springs at, dives at, tears at, attacks, and enters my soul.

Our lives shall not be sweated from
birth until life closes;
Hearts starve as well as bodies; give
us bread but give us roses!

Mean Little Shops

Hearts starve. You arrive at work in a cramped and mean little shop at seven in the morning. The boss has told you not to punch in until eight. He or his wife screams at you all day— "Hurry up, you idiot!" "Can't you sew a straight line?" "You're as clumsy as a dog." At five he punches out your time card, but you work until six or even later past evening and into night. Paid by the piece you have been a bit slower today, bothered by a puncture from a needle last week. If the multiplication was done you did not make the $5.15 an hour that is the legal minimum wage—though the official records will show you did because two of your hours are not recorded. The work is boring, repetitive, extremely uncomfortable, but it requires absolute attention. Should your thoughts stray for but a moment, should you wonder how your boy is doing in the first grade or if you might get nice weather to take a walk on Sunday, you will get injured. A robot may bring a stiff fender to a hard chassis, but as yet only a human hand can guide two limp pieces of fabric to be machine-sewn together in an arc or a tight corner.

Hearts Starve. When things are busy you will do this six days a week. You might work later than six o'clock in the evening. Then you might consider yourself lucky. Overtime is an opportunity to get another few dollars. You need them all. Rent takes most of what you get.

Hearts Starve. You have to use the toilet, but the washroom makes you nauseous and you are scared of the dark corridor and of catching some disease. The bathroom is filthy. The boss screams if you take enough time to try to clean it yourself.

"Cheap Unethical Clothes," cartoon by Stan Eales. www.CartoonStock.com.

Hearts Starve. There is a course for finishing high school at night in the neighborhood, but you never know when the overtime will come. You can't plan. If you say no to overtime you'll get fired. Will it always be like this? Can you ever breathe free?

The Demands of Fashion

Throughout the developed world, in Europe and North America, closets of clothing are stuffed with the changing demands of fashion. We slaves to fashion rarely wear out clothes in the physical sense: Instead, we grow tired of them. The next new thing adorns our bodies in each season. Thousands of commercial messages remind us in each season that we are perceived as we dress. How devastating it is to be told one is dressed "so eighties." As we are slaves to fashion as consumers so too are the producers. The flood of clothing demanded by consumerist culture is not necessarily paid for with a flood of new purchasing power: Clothing costs less as a portion of family budgets now than it did a generation ago. In New York and Bangladesh, in Los Angeles and Managua, hearts starve for the finer things in life as we slaves to fashion reap the product of those enslaved to fashion.

In January 1912 textile workers in Lawrence, Massachusetts, struck against a cut in their pay. The mill owners had lowered their pay in response to a Massachusetts law that reduced the workweek from fifty-six to fifty-four hours.

The workers were mainly immigrants, the largest number Italian. They were considered unskilled. The craft-oriented labor movement of the time thought these workers, many of them women, could not be organized. But the radical Industrial Workers of the World—the Wobblies of fame and song—were successful in organizing the women across ethnic and linguistic lines. A hard strike ensued, immortalized in a stirring, evocative painting by the artist Ralph Fasanella.

The women took the lead in the strike. They were set upon with violence. They had to send their children away to protect them—and by doing so they won sympathetic hearts to their cause as photographs of the children stepping down from trains, gazing out at strange cities, were carried in the newspapers of the day. The workers suffered betrayal, and attempts were made to frame them through outrageous schemes. Their Italian leaders were charged with the murder of Alice LoPezzo when police killed her. They maintained their unity and their dignity and finally in March 1912 won their demands.

Fully Human

The Lawrence strike began less than two years after the end of the "Uprising of the Twenty Thousand" shirtwaist makers in New York. The uprising was the largest ever industrial action by women at that point, and the Lawrence strike continued the story—immigrant women fighting for their rights. Even today, in New York's labor lore, the 1910 "Great Revolt" of sixty thousand largely male cloakmakers is a story somehow subordinated to that of the women.

As Abraham Lincoln put it, "The mystic chords of memory" call forth "the better angels of our nature." We seem to need the story of those women to tell us something or perhaps instruct us about ourselves. And so, for many years now, we have come to believe that during one of their marches the Lawrence textile workers carried a sign that, by this *act* of constructively remembering, has become the special emblem of women workers and of all who strive for dignity in their labor. Many speakers and writers have passed on the cultural memory that a Lawrence sign read, "*We want bread and roses too.*" Such a sentiment reminds us that those poor immigrant laborers—in Lawrence or in New York or in Los Angeles this morning as you glance at this page—were not just victims, not merely recipients of the good conscience of their allies, not merely reflexes of a market demand for clothing and fashion. They were fully human, with fully noble hopes and dreams even in their miserable stinking shops at six o'clock in the morning on cold days. The enslaved yearn for the finer and better things of life.

Memory has joined the Lawrence strikers to James Oppenheim's poem "Bread and Roses." Yet there is no evidence that the sign "We want bread and roses too" was ever carried by a Lawrence striker. Most recently [the late scholar] Jim Zwick discovered Oppenheim's poem was written and published *before* the Lawrence strike (in December, 1911), and he thinks the origin is in a Chicago garment strike in 1909–10.

The oppressed and exploited have always wanted not just tomorrow's bread but Sunday's roses too. The big struggles of working people involve "the individual awakening of 'illiterates' and 'scum' to an original, personal conception of society and the realization of the dignity and the rights of their part in it." When Rose Schneiderman, a garment worker unionist and suffrage campaigner, the great orator after the Triangle fire of 1911, gave a series of 1912 lectures on behalf of voting rights for women, she used the slogan to emphasize the need for working-class women to have a voice in public life.

The International Ladies' Garment Workers' Union (ILGWU, or ILG) sponsored a Broadway musical, *Pajama*

Game (beginning in 1954), which addressed the question of the meaning of small advances from a worker's point of view. "Seven and a Half Cents" is a song about an hourly raise. Trivial, perhaps. But as the song says, "Give it to me every hour of every day. . . . Soon I'll be livin' like a king." Well, if not a king or queen, then, anyhow, as Woody Guthrie said about Pete Seeger's vision for America, "All union, all free, all singing."

No Better Off

Hearts Starve. Around the world sewing machine operators toil day after day. In China's privately owned export factories they may work twenty-seven of thirty days, eleven hours a day. Economists and journalists from the West seem to be impressed that the apparel toilers of the developing countries are better off than indentured prostitutes or their sisters who remain on farms without electricity. They are not better off for long.

After ten years or perhaps a bit more, they return to the villages. They leave behind a mountain of jeans, a skyscraper of blouses, icebergs of fleece, and *Titanic*-sized piles of silk ties. An Everest of dress shirts anchors continents of sneakers. Then they are gone. There are hardly any forty-year-olds in China's export factories or in the export processing zones of the developing world. Spent and discarded, the women move on.

Hearts Starve. As I end my writing of this work of fealty to family and tradition, the U.S. Census is releasing the new figures for immigration in the decade from 1990 to 2000. It is as we knew. This has been the greatest era of immigration in our history. Just as the wave of immigrants at the turn of the twentieth century first brought the ready-to-wear clothing business to our shores, the Russian Jews and the Italians, the sewing machine operators and the cutters, so now Hispanic and Asian migrants populate the shops and factories of the rag trade. It has ever been the merciless devourer of immigrants. It takes whole lives but doesn't say thanks. Those Jewish and Catholic and Orthodox immigrants from Southern and Eastern Europe were different from the Protestant and Western Europeans who preceded them. And now still darker hued people come to make our dresses and slacks, and they are also different from the Europeans who preceded them. But not so different.

Hearts Starve. They come to earn a decent life. To avoid a bomb or a bullet late at night. To make a safe place for their children and, if they are very lucky, to have a moment or two to rest in the sun. They are just like us. They are our grandparents and parents and great-grandparents. We owe them what we owe them.

This book [*Slaves to Fashion: Poverty and Abuse in the New Sweatshops*] has a lot of numbers in it. But it has only one vision. Behind every chart or table and fact and policy is a woman or a man at a sewing machine and a cutting table. Whose hearts starve.

As we go marching, marching in
the beauty of the day,
A million darkened kitchens, a
thousand mill lofts gray,
Are touched with all the radiance
that a sudden sun discloses,
For the people hear us singing:
"Bread and roses! Bread and roses!"
As we go marching, marching, we
battle too for men,
For they are women's children, and
we mother them again.
Our lives shall not be sweated from
birth until life closes;
Hearts starve as well as bodies; give
us bread but give us roses!
—James Oppenheim, 1911

> *"We are convinced that we have an opportunity to contribute to better working conditions for all the hundreds of thousands of people who make our products."*

Some Fashion Companies Monitor and Improve Working Conditions in Factories

H&M

H&M is a multinational clothing company based in Sweden. In the following viewpoint, H&M declares that it aims to improve and maintain the working conditions of the people who make its products. According to the company, this includes ensuring that factories are clean and safe, banning child labor, guaranteeing fair work hours, protecting wages, and reserving workers' right to freedom of association. These goals are achieved through regular and unannounced audits and requiring suppliers to improve as needed, H&M states. Furthermore, it insists that child labor is not common in the garment industry.

H&M, "Supply Chain Working Conditions," March 2009. Copyright © H&M Hennes & Mauritz AB 2009. Reproduced by permission. www.hm.com.

As you read, consider the following questions:

1. According to H&M, in which cases does it reject a supplier?

2. What are the duties of its auditors, as stated by H&M?

3. What does the company claim to do when it discovers an underage worker?

H&M sources clothes and other products from about 800 suppliers who in turn use subcontractors. In all, around 2,700 production units and hundreds of thousands of people are involved in the manufacture of our products.

Our choice of countries of manufacture places particularly high demands on us. We are aware of the risk of human rights violations and non-compliance with local labour law and internationally agreed labour standards. At the same time, we are convinced that we have an opportunity to contribute to better working conditions for all the hundreds of thousands of people who make our products.

Our Code of Conduct

H&M does not have any factories of its own. Instead we buy all our garments and other goods from around 800 suppliers, primarily in Asia and Europe.

Since we do not have direct control over this production we have drawn up guidelines for our suppliers, which together form our Code of Conduct.

This Code of Conduct is based on the UN [United Nations] Convention on the Rights of the Child and ILO's [International Labour Organization's] conventions on working conditions and rights at work. It is there so that we can be sure that our products are produced under good working conditions.

The Code includes requirements concerning:

- working environment

- a ban on child labour

- fire safety

- working hours

- wages

- freedom of association

Factory Audits

Agreement with suppliers. Each supplier undertakes to abide by H&M's Code of Conduct. Not all our suppliers meet every one of our requirements from the start, but they must commit themselves to implementing the changes required to do so in order to be accepted as a supplier to H&M. Certain basic requirements must always be met. For example, a supplier who refuses to allow trade unions or has employees who are younger than the law and our Code of Conduct allows will not be accepted as a supplier. We also require that our suppliers tell us all the subcontractors that may be used for the manufacture of H&M products, so that we can be sure that we have control over where our clothes are produced.

Factory audits. We employ staff at our production offices to check that H&M's suppliers and their subcontractors carry out the improvements necessary to meet our requirements. We now have 19 offices in the biggest production markets and a total of around 60 auditors whose full-time job is to check that our Code of Conduct is being observed.

Our auditors work their way through a form containing over 300 points. They interview the company management and employees, inspect all factory premises and check documentation such as payroll reports and time cards.

Reporting inspection results. After each audit we collate the results in a report, specifying the areas where improvements are needed, and the supplier must draw up an action plan within a specified period. The auditors then follow up whether the improvements have been made. We carry out both pre-arranged and unannounced inspections.

Thanks to IT [information technology] support, both the production offices and the head office always have access to information on different factories. The buyers who send out orders can also access summaries of the results of the audits, which can make the choice of supplier easier.

Long-term relationships with suppliers. We try to build up long-term relationships with our suppliers. To help our suppliers understand and live up to the requirements of our Code of Conduct we provide the opportunity for them to participate in workshops on international labour standards and how these are implemented. These workshops are usually organised by H&M, but sometimes by external partners such as the American organisation, BSR (Business for Social Responsibility), of which H&M is a member.

A Day in the Life of an Auditor

Payal Jain and Tobias Fischer are two of around 60 auditors working for H&M. Their job is to inspect working conditions at H&M's suppliers and to check that the ILO core conventions and H&M's Code of Conduct are being respected. Payal and Tobias work together, visiting suppliers in and around New Delhi.

It is early in the morning when Tobias Fischer and Payal Jain arrive at the factory gates in their car. No one knows they are coming today. Tobias and Payal wear H&M ID badges so that the guards and the factory staff know who they are. Six months ago, auditors carried out a comprehensive inspection of the working conditions at the factory and Payal and Tobias are here today to find out whether the supplier has achieved the short-term goals set during that visit.

Code of conduct is the starting point. Like all of H&M's suppliers, the factory has signed up to a cooperation agreement—H&M's code of conduct—promising to comply with local legislation and H&M's requirements regarding the working environment. The agreement also contains a provision stipulating that H&M's auditors can make unannounced visits. "We carry out an extensive audit whenever we start working with a new supplier. This takes between two and seven days. We work with the factory managers to identify key areas for improvement, and decide on a plan of action. The plan contains both long-term and short-term goals and sets out how the goals should be achieved, who will be responsible and when the work should be completed," explains Tobias.

Unannounced visits. Payal and Tobias enter the factory and ask for the manager. He greets them and accompanies them on a tour of the factory. Since H&M first introduced the code of conduct in India in 1998, the auditors have made repeated visits to the factories. "To begin with the factory owners were a little unused to the idea of being inspected like this. Now they understand that unannounced visits are part and parcel of the way we work, and few are surprised when we turn up out of the blue," says Payal.

Improvements implemented. The auditors check the fire escapes and discuss safety routines with a factory representative. These include the provision of fire alarms, emergency exits and fire extinguishers, but also cover aspects such as making sure the factory is always clean and tidy and that there are a sufficient number of good, clean toilets. The working environment is important, both for the workers' well-being and for the quality of the clothing produced. Payal notes that the working environment has improved considerably since the last visit. In the past there had been problems with material remnants from the cutting machines and thread from the production area being left lying around. Now the factory has employed more cleaners, supplied suitable tools and equipment and introduced better routines. The factory is clean and is now a safer and more pleasant place for the employees to work.

Overtime a problem. When Payal and Tobias have finished the factory inspection they go to the supplier's office to examine the paperwork relating to the employees. They check payroll information and employee records, and see how much overtime has been worked. Recently, some departments at the factory were understaffed. This hampered production and led to excessive amounts of overtime being worked. Having inspected the time cards, payroll information and production records, Tobias and Payal can confirm that the overtime has been reduced, but it is still above the legal limit. The supplier will have to continue following the action plan.

Then it's time to drive back to H&M's offices in New Delhi to document the visit and to report back to the CSR [corporate social responsibility] department at the head office in Sweden.

Influencing attitudes. The auditor's job is far from simple because it involves influencing other people's attitudes and behaviour. Payal explains: "It can be quite a tough challenge to persuade suppliers that they have a lot to gain from H&M's Code of Conduct and the cooperation with us. I try and get them to see that it can make their employees more motivated and may well even increase productivity. We want the suppliers to strive for lasting improvements because they can see the benefits for themselves, not just because the buyer says they have to. Their task, as I see it, is to put us out of a job."

What Do We Do If We Find Child Labour Being Used?

If we discover people who are below the statutory minimum age for working we always act in their best interests.

Agreement on a good solution. On the few occasions on which we have discovered underage workers at our suppliers

Made in Downtown LA

American Apparel is rising fast in just about all the things that matter: quality of product, service, sales and development of its workforce. When companies go to extremes to lower costs, American Apparel invests in its employees, providing competitive—if not higher wages than similar companies—plus generous benefits that extend to a concern for employees' health and welfare.

Chamber Voice, "Doin' It Right,"
September 2003. http://americanapparel.net.

we have acted in accordance with our policy. In cooperation with the supplier we have tried to find a solution that is in the best interests of the child. The family is contacted and in most cases the family accepts that the child should continue with some kind of education until he or she is 15 years old, or the lawful age for working in the country in question (but not lower than 14 years). Wages continue to be paid during the study period so that the family does not lose its income. In certain cases an older member of the household has been offered work instead of the child. In a few cases the child and the family concerned preferred the solution of the child returning to his or her home, which may be hundreds of kilometres away. In such cases the supplier has made a one-off payment to compensate for the cost of the ticket and loss of wages.

A better future. On each individual occasion our ultimate aim is to help the child to a better future. Our policy in respect of child labour must not result in children being dismissed from factories without any follow-up, with the risk that he or she will instead end up in heavier and more dan-

111

gerous work or—in the worst case—in prostitution. In order to assure ourselves of this in the best way possible we have built up networks of local contacts such as schools and voluntary organisations, who know the local circumstances and can help us to find good solutions.

Age assessment. We also have contacts with doctors who can help us to judge the age of those who we think look particularly young during our factory audits. Often no documentation is found and in the worst case neither the families nor the child knows how old he or she is. Lack of documentation is a big problem and we are constantly working on getting our suppliers to improve their routines, so that they can give a serious assurance that everyone who is working in their factory has reached the lawful age for employment. We require some kind of proof of age to be checked on employment or, if there is no such proof, for a doctor to establish his or her approximate age.

If we find child labour more than once. Since we take child labour very seriously we are very strict in respect of our suppliers. The first time a child is discovered working for a supplier or his subcontractor we demand that the supplier takes his responsibilities seriously and together with H&M finds a solution that is in the best interests of the child. If we find child labour being employed by the same supplier—or one of his subcontractors—on a second occasion we cease our cooperation with the supplier for good. This has also occurred on a few occasions.

Toward Improved Conditions

How far have we come? Real improvements have been achieved since we started these factory inspections in 1998.

In the early days we found that the factories were often unclean and in poor condition. Demands for better lighting, ventilation and cleaning routines made a real difference to the working environment.

Fire safety often left something to be desired. Fire extinguishers and emergency exits were missing. There were no fire alarms or evacuation plans and no fire drills were carried out. Now that H&M and other buyers have been setting requirements of better safety for a few years there has been a real improvement in fire safety in the factories.

To check aspects such as wages and working hours, we started off by examining the documents that existed in the factories. Fairly soon we realized that first we had to get our suppliers to introduce meaningful reporting systems. Once this had been done we were able to effectively check that the staff were getting the wages to which they were entitled. This work is naturally dependant on having an open relationship between the suppliers and H&M. It is essential to know the actual circumstances if we are to get to grips with any problems and find lasting solutions.

Interviews with our suppliers' employees are now a natural part of our follow-up work. It is mainly by listening to the workers that we have come to understand the importance of educating them regarding their rights. A number of projects in countries such as India and Bangladesh have been aimed at precisely this.

We also focus on communication between management and workers in the factories and systems for raising grievances and putting forward views. The aim is for the factories to create conditions in which the workers can themselves affect their working situation.

Child labour is not common. Despite the attention that it has had in the media, child labour has proved to be a very rare occurrence. For many years the export industry has been aware that Western companies will not accept child labour. Nonetheless, we have discovered a few children in the 13 to 15 age range during our inspections, generally due to sloppy employment routines or because the children produced fake ID documents. Since establishing the real age of everyone working at the factories is problematic, all documentation that exists about the employees is checked. The date of employment is compared with the date of birth to check that nobody was employed at too low an age, even if they had reached a lawful age for employment by the time of the inspection.

Periodical Bibliography

The following articles have been selected to supplement the diverse views presented in this chapter.

Michael Baker	"The Pain in Spain Offers Retail Re-Frame," *Sydney Morning Herald*, February 9, 2009.
Kate Betts, Bruce Crumley, James Graff, Helen Gibson, Neil Gough, and Jeff Israely	"The Purse-Party Blues," *TIME*, August 2, 2004.
T.A. Frank	"Confessions of a Sweatshop Inspector," *Washington Monthly*, April 2008.
Susannah Frankel	"The Real Cost of Fashion—A Special Report," *The Independent*, November 16, 2007.
Richard Gray	"The American Dream," *Fashion Inc*, Spring/Summer 2007.
Mark Holgate	"Why Less Is More," *Vogue*, November 2007.
Marc Karimzadeh	"An Overheated System: Frenzied Fashion Seasons Propel Debate on Change," *WWD*, February 8, 2007.
Nicholas D. Kristof	"Where Sweatshops Are a Dream," *New York Times*, April 6, 2009.
Andrew Malone	"Revealed: The True Cost of Buying Cheap Fake Goods," *Daily Mail*, July 29, 2007.
Susie Mesure	"Fashion Must Clean up Its Act, or Be Left Behind with Last Season's Look," *New Statesman*, October 8, 2007.

CHAPTER 3

Is the Fashion Industry
Appropriately Regulated?

Chapter Preface

From the gamine slenderness of the 1960s to the "heroin chic" rage of the 1990s, fashion's ideal of thinness has been a lightning rod for controversy. At five feet, ten inches tall and weighing one hundred and ten pounds, the typical model today would have a body mass index (BMI) of 15.8, well below the recommended range of 18.5–25. Some of modeling's most recognizable faces and famous bodies—Naomi Campbell, Kate Moss, and Gisele Bundchen—have BMIs hovering around sixteen. One point less is indicative of starvation, malnutrition, or an eating disorder.

During the mid-2000s, the shocking deaths of several models rocked the fashion industry. In August 2006, Luisel Ramos, a twenty-two-year-old from Uruguay, collapsed and died of heart failure after exiting the runway at a show. She had a BMI of 14.5 and was severely malnourished, having subsisted on lettuce and diet soft drinks for three months. The following November, Ana Carolina Reston, a twenty-one-year-old Brazilian represented by top-tier agencies such as Ford and Elite, died from complications resulting from anorexia and bulimia. At the time of her death, she was five feet, eight inches tall and weighed eighty-eight pounds. In February 2007, Ramos's eighteen-year-old sister and up-and-coming catwalker, Eliana, also died from malnutrition, fueling speculation that she too starved herself for fashion.

The month after the death of Luisel Ramos, the Association of Fashion Designers of Spain banned models with BMIs less than eighteen and under sixteen years of age from fashion shows. "The restrictions could be quite a shock to the fashion world at the beginning but I'm sure it's important as far as health is concerned,"[1] insists Leonor Pérez Pita, who directs Madrid fashion week. As a consequence, Brazil, Argentina, and, after protracted dialogue, Italy enacted similar bans. By

July 2009, France, England, and the United States, home to three of the "Big Four" fashion weeks, have yet to follow suit. Storm Models founder Sarah Doukas, who had originally scouted Kate Moss, maintains that such restrictions are unnecessary: "It is useless to talk about BMIs. Who knows what that means apart from your doctor? It depends on different body types."[2] In the following chapter, experts and commentators investigate both sides of this issue and other calls for regulation in the fashion industry.

Notes

1. BBC News, September 13, 2006.
2. Karen Kay, *Daily Mail*, September 18, 2006.

> *"The lack of protection of fashion designs is eroding innovation and hampering the competitiveness of American fashion designers."*

Fashion Designers Need Copyright Protection

Alain Coblence

The Design Piracy Prohibition Act was proposed in 2006 and intends to expand copyright law to include fashion designs for the duration of three years. In the following viewpoint, Alain Coblence supports the passage of the bill. Without copyright protection, fashion designers' creations will continue to be knocked off overseas as soon as they hit the runways and fake luxury goods without labels will still be permitted to enter the United States, argues Coblence. Contrary to opponents' claims, he states that frivolous lawsuits will not proliferate and innovation will flourish under the law. The author is counsel to the Council of Fashion Designers of America (CFDA) and helped draft the Design Piracy Prohibition Act.

As you read, consider the following questions:

1. According to Alain Coblence, how will three-year protection benefit fashion designers?

2. How does Coblence respond to the argument that copying promotes innovation in fashion design?

3. How does the author define piracy?

The Design Piracy Prohibition Act, proposed last year [2006] by U.S. Rep. Bob Goodlatte (R-Roanoke, Va.), was reintroduced this year to both houses of Congress after several months of review by a subcommittee chaired by U.S. Rep. Howard Berman (D-San Fernando Valley, Calif.). The proposed law would extend copyright protection beyond existing coverage of textile prints, patterns and surface design to include original apparel and accessories. If passed, the law would grant copyright protection to original apparel and clothing for a period of three years, in effect giving designers and manufacturers a legal avenue to maintain some exclusivity to their creations. The three-year protection was intended to give the original designer time to bring the look to market and then be able to knock it off for a subsequent collection or a lower-priced diffusion line before the design enters the public domain. The Design Piracy bill has attracted some well-known supporters, including Council of Fashion Designers of America president Diane von Furstenberg, designer Nicole Miller and *Project Runway* star Tim Gunn. But there are many in the fashion industry who oppose the law, including California Fashion Association executive director Ilse Metchek and many California-based copyright attorneys and financial industry executives. On one side of the debate are the opponents, who say the law will halt the flow of trends from the top echelon of design down to the mass market. The proponents say fashion trends will still permeate the market, but now designers will have a legal means to protect their designs from being copied as soon as—or sometime before—they hit the retail floor.

California Apparel News executive editor Alison A. Nieder invited two experts on either side of the debate to argue their case regarding the law.

The recently proposed law extending copyright protection to fashion clothing and accessories will, if passed, give designers a means to protect themselves from pirated—or knockoff—copies of their work.

Today more than ever, it is innovation—not production—that fuels the American economy. At a time when the American fashion industry has become a world leader, the lack of protection of fashion designs is eroding innovation and hampering the competitiveness of American fashion designers, whose creations are daily and openly knocked off.

The development of new technologies in the last few years has made it considerably worse. Via the Internet, counterfeiters and pirates in China and in undeveloped low-wage countries have immediate access to all fashion creations the minute they are viewed by the American public. As a result of these new technologies, knock-off garments are now often marketed weeks before the originals.

Under our present law, the copyright of a fabric design is well-established and well-protected. Even though the design of a dress or a handbag entails similar artistic creation, in the United States, unlike in Europe or Japan, the law does not give any protection to fashion designers.

Furthermore, although counterfeits—pirated designs with a fake label—are prohibited, millions of pirated goods are allowed to enter this country every year without the label, only to have fake labels affixed later in the United States. Thus piracy constitutes the linchpin of counterfeiting—it is counterfeiting without the label—and our country stands alone as the Trojan Horse of global counterfeiting.

The Proposed Law

The bill addresses the following issues:

- It adopts what, in 1998, Congress provided in the statutory protection of "useful designs" except that it only seeks three years' protection instead of 10. (By way of comparison, Europe protects registered fashion designs for 25 years.)

- It applies exclusively to those original designs that are truly unique, and it recognizes the fact that inspiration and trends are part of the industry's creative process. The law reads: "A design cannot be granted protection if it is staple or commonplace, standard, prevalent or ordinary, or different only in insignificant details or elements."

- It will not protect any design that has been made public prior to the law's enactment. Thus, it will prevent designers from claiming copyrights over styles and features invented by others.

- Its protection provides exclusions for sellers and distributors who act without knowledge, and there are other broad general exclusions for acts without general knowledge.

The Impact of the Legislation

Opponents of this bill have raised the specter of a proliferation of lawsuits. Naturally no area of intellectual property has a bright line rule that distinguishes between what is a copy and what is not. In the case of fashion design, it is no different from a song or a book. That being said, there are several features of the bill that will avoid frivolous lawsuits, such as

A Form of Creative Expression

While in the early days of U.S. copyright only books and maps were eligible for registration, the scope of protection has since increased to include painting, sculpture, textile patterns, and even jewelry design—but not clothing.

Why has clothing been excluded from protection? The problem lies in a reductionistic view of fashion as solely utilitarian. Current U.S. law understands clothing only in terms of its usefulness as a means of covering the body, regardless of how original it might be. Surface decoration aside, the plainest T-shirt and the most fanciful item of apparel receive exactly the same treatment under copyright law. In fact, a T-shirt with a simple drawing on the front would receive *more* protection than an elaborate ball gown that is the product of dozens of preliminary sketches, hours of fittings, and days of detailed stitching and adjustment before it is finally complete. The legal fiction that even the most conceptual clothing design is merely functional prevents the protection of original designs.

Fashion, however, is not just about covering the body—it is about creative expression, which is exactly what copyright is supposed to protect. Historians and other scholars make an important distinction between clothing and fashion. "Clothing" is a general term for "articles of dress that cover the body," while "fashion" is a form of creative expression.

Susan Scafaldi, Statement on H.R. 5055,
U.S. House of Representatives, Committee on the
Judiciary, Subcommittee on Courts, the Internet,
and Intellectual Property, *July 27, 2006.*

the exclusion of design lacking in originality, which will be made part of the public domain. The best answer to those afraid of a proliferation of lawsuits is to refer to what happens in Europe. The level of litigation there is extremely low because the highly protective legislation acts as a deterrent, and very few cases are brought to court.

Opponents of the bill have also argued that this new protection would stifle the growth of the U.S. industry. There is nothing further from the truth as demonstrated by the unique level of creativity and prosperity of the fashion industry in France, Italy and Japan, where protection has been so strong for decades. It is also evident in this country; the design of jewelry has been protected for more than 50 years and that industry is thriving.

The theory that copying actually promotes innovation of designer clothing—because the more common a look becomes, the more the fashion-conscious seek out the next thing—is an insult to common sense as well as to the most elementary decency. To claim that piracy accelerates the fashion cycle is like saying that theft should be encouraged because, by necessity of replacement, it would increase the nation's industrial output.

Some opponents of the bill have also claimed that this bill would have the effect of stifling the access of a large segment of consumers to lower-priced garments. In fact, great American fashion design is available at every price point. Mass retailers are increasingly licensing designers to create collections for their stores. This protects designers while making fashion available at affordable prices to consumers. The bill encourages this trend and seeks to balance the scales for us all.

Pirates, on the other hand, steal American designs, make low-quality copies in foreign factories with cheap labor and import them into the United States to compete with original American fashion. This is currently legal under U.S. law. The lack of protective laws in our country has made it a haven for piracy.

Piracy is counterfeiting without the label, and counterfeiting is a breeding ground for organized crime, while relying on child labor and funding terrorism. This, more than anything else, is why it is crucial to close this criminal loophole.

This bill must be enacted to protect our fashion industry, to promote American design, to harmonize U.S. law with that of our closest trade partners and to fight against counterfeiting.

"*Copying that harms individual designers may be a boon to the industry as a
whole.*"

Fashion Designers Do Not
Need Copyright Protection

Julian Sanchez

*Introduced in 2006, the Design Piracy Prohibition Act aims to
extend copyright protection to fashion designs for three years. In
the following viewpoint, Julian Sanchez alleges that such legislation is unnecessary. He states that counterfeiting labels and logos
and copying unique graphics and fabric prints are already out-
lawed. Moreover, the author upholds that designers frequently
"interpret" or pay "homage" to other designers' work, so most
current styles have precedent. Giving copyright protection to
fashion designs would end the copying that drives trends and the
demand for new styles, he claims. Sanchez is a contributing editor to* Reason.

As you read, consider the following questions:

1. What three emerging trends have prompted the call for
   fashion design copyright law, in the author's view?

2. How does the author describe Gwen Stefani's label?

3. According to Julian Sanchez, how does piracy in fashion differ than in other industries?

As Fashion Week in Manhattan draws to a close, spring's style commandments are as clear as [late actor] Charlton Heston's baritone: Out with exposed flesh; in with bright palettes, color blocking, and minute details like pintucks and pleats. But while high-end designers dominated the runways this week, those too penurious [frugal] for Proenza Schouler need not resort to sackcloth and ashes: A small army of knock-off specialists are already translating the tablets handed down from sartorial Sinai into cheap-chic for "fast fashion" retailers like Zara, H&M, and Forever 21. Many couturiers, though, regard these woven images as abominations nearly as foul as brown shoes with black slacks. They're urging Congress to issue an injunction of its own: Thou shalt not knock off.

Peddling counterfeit labels or logos is already illegal, of course, and copyright law protects any graphic images, including unique fabric prints, that are incorporated into a garment. But in the United States, at least, the design of the garment itself has traditionally been beyond the reach of intellectual property (IP) law—largely on the grounds that fashion serves functional rather than aesthetic purposes.

The Council of Fashion Designers of America [CFDA] is lobbying to change that. The industry group is pushing the Design Piracy Prohibition Act, which would create a special, limited three-year copyright in fashion designs, with penalties of $250,000 or $5 per copy for violations. The bill has been under consideration in the House since last year [2006], and in August [2007] it was joined by a Senate version introduced by New York Democrat Chuck Schumer and eight co-sponsors.

In an industry rife with "interpretation" and "homage," designers had long adopted a relatively *laissez-faire* [opposing government intervention in economic affairs] attitude toward downmarket copying. Three overlapping trends have begun to change that. The first is the increased speed with which the Internet—and, less obviously, but more importantly, flexible supply chains and just-in-time inventory—allows at least rough copies to appear in stores at the same time as their high-end templates (rather than a season behind the curve). The second is the rise of "masstige" lines at such retailers as Target and Kohl's, designed by the likes of Marc Jacobs and Vera Wang but aimed at the mass market.

Finally, there's the popularity of "high-low" aesthetics. As MIT cultural anthropologist Grant McCracken has observed, people typically construct consistent identities by clustering their consumption on one market tier. But those lines are beginning to blur, as mid-market buyers seek to accent ordinary outfits with one high-end accessory, and affluent fashion plates seem more willing to mix and match budget and couture elements. Where once the knockoff buyer was seen as "not our customer," in the delicate phrasing of renowned designer Tom Ford, many are beginning to see the copies as competition. And masstige collaboration between bold-faced names and discount shops is making some retailers more reluctant to alienate designers by openly opposing new IP rules.

That's not to say there's consensus: Industry sources say there's wide agreement that the current forms of the Design Piracy Prohibition Act need plenty of work before they're ready for prime time. And even many designers have their doubts about letting the law police imitation. Wunderkind designer Zac Posen has helped lobby for the bill, but he also tells Reuters, "It's a very fine line of what is a copy and what is inspiration."

The law asks whether a garment or accessory is "closely and substantially similar in overall visual appearance to a protected design"—a question the courts answer using several standards that may vary from circuit to circuit, according to attorney Eric Osterberg, who literally wrote the book on copyright's "substantial similarity" standard. In some cases, the reaction of the "ordinary observer" defines similarity, whereas in others the eye of the "more discerning" expert provides the benchmark.

Osterberg isn't convinced the problem is any more insoluble in fashion than it is in music or fiction, but he allows that there will be plenty of uncertainty, at least initially. As the legendary jurist Learned Hand wrote in 1960, "The test for infringement of a copyright is of necessity vague. . . . In the case of designs, which are addressed to the aesthetic sensibilities of an observer, the test is, if possible, even more intangible." Still more so, he might have added, when we expect different collections to follow the same seasonal trends.

Even clothes that buck the current style typically have historical precedent. "There isn't a thing in *Women's Wear Daily* right now, from the new collections, that I haven't seen before," says Ilse Metchek, executive director of the California Fashion Association, which opposes the law. She believes fast fashion firms will generally be able to find a safe harbor by mining the design archives for the original inspirations behind this season's runway looks.

Much innovation in fashion, however, is drawn not from catalogues, but from what amateurs on the street are doing. Pop star-cum-designer Gwen Stefani is suing Forever 21 for infringing the trademark of her Harajuku Lovers line with a logo she claims is too close to her own. But as the name advertises, Stefani's own designs are modeled on the anime-inflected dress of teenagers who hang out in Tokyo's Harajuku district.

Thorny as these problems may be, a deeper question is whether it's even proper to frame the debate as being about "piracy," which implicitly suggests an analogy with illicit copying of software, music, and movies. One way "piracy" rhetoric has clouded the issue is by obscuring the difference between knockoffs and counterfeits. A press release from the office of

A Looming Litigation Nightmare

Every time a designer wants to work with a current trend, she will be afraid that such a new look is somehow "owned" by another designer. (Would every fraction of an inch of a lower hemline belong to a different designer?) And as I understand the law, even designs that were created before the new law aren't entirely safe. My understanding is that someone could claim a copyright even in a design that's been around a while—they'll just claim that they didn't copy it from the pre-existing design but re-invented it themselves! What's clear to me is that if this bill passes we've got a looming litigation nightmare in the fashion industry.

Steve Maiman, Testimony in Opposition to H.R. 2033, U.S. House of Representatives, Committee on the Judiciary, Subcommittee on Courts, the Internet, and Intellectual Property, *February 14, 2008.*

Virginia Republican Bob Goodlatte, a sponsor of the House version of the bill, invokes Customs and Border Protection statistics showing that "counterfeiting merchandise, as a whole, is responsible for the loss of 750,000 American jobs" and "between \$200 and \$250 billion in sales." But counterfeits are illegal under current law, and banning imitations by legitimate retailers may drive consumers, not to the designer originals, but to the black-market bags and blouses that have been linked with funding terrorism.

There are also important differences between the way copying works in fashion and the way it works in other industries. A bootleg copy of a CD or a computer program is a near-perfect substitute for the genuine article: Sony and Microsoft worry about piracy because they fear the copies will directly displace sales. Designers, however, seem at least as concerned about dilution as displacement: They worry couture consumers will flee goods that lose their aura of exclusivity, like [the Dr. Seuss characters] Sneetches rubbing the stars from their bellies.

An extreme example of this can be found in the case of Burberry, which saw its British sales decline when counterfeits of the clothier's distinctive plaid became the unofficial uniform of England's gauche "chav" culture. But if this is the concern, fashion copyrights begin to look less like conventional IP and more like a modern analogue of the Elizabethan sumptuary laws, which kept class boundaries distinct by specifying who was entitled to wear which fabrics: purple silk for the royal family; gold cloth for ranks above viscount; and velvet for the sons of barons.

Even when the ubiquity of a style harms the sales of particular garments by widely-copied designers, however, it need not lower sales for high-end fashion as a whole. Instead, it may cause lateral displacement, as the fashion elite seek out less common looks. That could yield what legal scholars Kal Raustiala and Christopher Sprigman have dubbed "The Piracy Paradox": Copying that harms individual designers may be a boon to the industry as a whole, as it popularizes trends and then burns them out, speeding up the fashion cycle and spurring demand for new styles. "When a successful restaurant opens up on a street that's never had a restaurant before, there's a way in which the second business is parasitic on the first," says Raustiala. "But in the United States, we call that capitalism and competition."

As the copyright office's own analysis noted, there's no data showing that knockoffs have done any net harm to high fashion, and the explosive growth of fast fashion has coexisted with a massive luxury boom. Betsy Fisher, who owns an eponymous clothing boutique in Washington D.C., suggests this may be because knockoffs create "fashion groupies," serving as a kind of gateway drug to couture for the teens who are flocking to fast fashion.

Indeed: What about the children? Discussion of fashion copyrights tends to focus on the ambiguous effect knockoffs may have on high-end design houses. But consumers clearly love the aesthetic options provided by fast fashion, which the CFA's Metchek notes is highly dependent on retailers' ability to respond immediately to trendsetting movies, TV shows, and music videos. Designers themselves can meet some of that demand through masstige lines, but they are constrained by the need to avoid diluting their own cachet through over-exposure.

The booming growth of fast fashion retailers may also be giving a shot in the arm to flagging domestic apparel manu-factures, since the flexibility and fast turnaround their busi-ness model requires makes local production more attractive than offshore outsourcing. That's the path Zara has followed in Europe, where, perhaps ironically, fast fashion flourishes despite the existence of design copyright protection because couturiers have shown relatively little interest in filing and en-forcing claims (though some observers believe this is begin-ning to change).

The Constitution empowers Congress to create copyrights in order to "promote the progress of science and the useful arts," and often they do just that. But since fashion seems to be progressing nicely on its own, it's important to demon-strate empirically the need to alter the rules under which the industry has operated for two centuries. The presumption that designing garments involves less creativity than painting por-traits or composing symphonies may be misguided. But it would be no less misguided to assume that the restrictions on copying that nourish those art forms would be just as benefi-cial to fashion.

> "Although the fashion industry does not directly cause eating disorders, it does contribute greatly to our culture's perception of beauty."

Extremely Thin Models Should Be Banned from Fashion Shows

Academy for Eating Disorders

In the following viewpoint, the Academy of Eating Disorders (AED) declares that the entire fashion industry should follow Spain's 2006 ban on underweight models. The AED asserts that eating disorders such as anorexia and bulimia are caused by a combination of genetic and environmental factors and fashion is highly accountable for cultural perceptions of beauty. It offers guidelines for the industry to follow, which includes not only banning underweight models, but also screening for eating disorders and presenting different body types on catwalks, in advertisements, and in magazines. Headquartered in Illinois, the AED is an international organization for eating disorder treatment, research, and education.

As you read, consider the following questions:

1. How does the AED's president react to Spain's ban on underweight models in fashion shows?

2. Why does the AED recommend that models be at least sixteen years of age?

3. What photographic techniques should be banned, as stated by the AED?

The Academy for Eating Disorders, an international organization for eating disorder treatment, research and education professionals, calls for a global ban on the use of severely underweight models in fashion shows and in fashion magazines and encourages the industry to adopt a minimum acceptable height-to-weight ratio in keeping with the guidelines established by the World Health Organization.

"The unprecedented move of a major fashion show in Spain to impose weight minimums on its runway models, in line with World Health Organization guidelines, is a sign that the industry is starting to take responsibility," said AED president Eric van Furth, PhD, FAED, "but we need to take this a step further to include global action."

Eating disorders, such as anorexia nervosa and bulimia nervosa, are potentially life-threatening mental illnesses that primarily affect young women. Research shows that a combination of genetic and environmental factors triggers the onset of these devastating illnesses.

One such environmental factor is an emphasis on body shape and weight. Research indicates that the gap between the beauty ideal presented by the fashion industry and reality can have a negative effect on self-esteem. Many young women and men turn to dieting in an effort to live up to this beauty ideal. For those who are vulnerable, the combination of dieting and low self-esteem may lead to the development of an eating disorder.

Although the fashion industry does not directly cause eating disorders, it does contribute greatly to our culture's perception of beauty. . . .

Academy for Eating Disorders Position Statement on the Fashion Industry

Anorexia nervosa, bulimia nervosa, binge eating disorder and other related eating disorders are serious mental disorders. Anorexia nervosa has the highest mortality rate of any psychiatric illness. Eating disorders affect the physical, psychological, and social well-being of millions of people of all ages and their families. The Academy for Eating Disorders (AED) calls upon the fashion and beauty industries to protect the health and well-being of young workers.

The AED recommends the following:

- The AED urges the fashion industry to institute regular, yearly medical evaluations and developmentally-appropriate medical and psychological screening and assessments for all models.

- The AED is prepared to make developmentally appropriate eating disorders assessment readily available to models and referring physicians.

- The AED appeals to the fashion and beauty industries to follow the *Guidelines for the Fashion Industry*, as developed and published by the Academy for Eating Disorders, on January 9, 2007. The primary goal of these guidelines is to preserve the health and well-being of models worldwide.

- The AED will work with major eating disorder and health organizations, to collaborate with and support the fashion and beauty industries in their efforts to safeguard the health of young workers, to detect eating disorders, and [to] provide appropriate referrals when needed. . . .

"Clothes hang better on skinny models."

"Clothes hang better on skinny models," cartoon by Grizelda. www.CartoonStock.com.

Academy for Eating Disorders Guidelines for the Fashion Industry

- Adoption of an age threshold requiring that models be at least 16 years of age so as to reduce the pressure that adolescent girls feel to conform to the ultra-thin standard of female beauty.

- For women and men over the age of 18, adoption of a minimum body mass index threshold of 18.5 kg/m2, (e.g., a female model who is 5' 9" [1.75 m] must weigh more than 126 pounds [57.3 kg]), which recognizes that weight below this is considered underweight by the World Health Organization.

- For female and male models between the ages of 16 and 18, adoption of a minimum body mass index for age and sex equivalent to the 10th BMI percentile for age and sex (weight below this is considered under-weight by the Centers for Disease Control). For example, applying this criterion to a 16-year-old female model, the minimum required body mass index would be 17.4 kg/m2, for a male model 17.7 kg/m2. A 16-year-old female model who is 5' 9" [1.75 m] must weigh more than 117 pounds [53.3 kg].

• Adoption of an independent medical certification affirming that students who are aspiring models do not suffer from an eating disorder and/or related medical complications (see below).

• Development of action steps to identify models in need of intervention and appropriate and sensitive procedures for detection and referral.

• Discouragement of all non-healthy weight control behaviors throughout the industry (e.g., self-induced vomiting, use of laxatives, diuretics and diet pills). Increased educational initiatives aimed at student models and professional models, their agents and employers to reduce the multiple health risks of various unhealthy weight control behaviors.

• Provision of educational initiatives aimed at aspiring and working student models, professional models, their agents and employers to raise awareness of the multiple health risks of low weight and restricted nutritional intake. These health risks include irregularity or cessation of menses, bradycardia (low heart rate)/irregular heart beat, electrolyte imbalances, dizziness/fainting spells, sudden cardiac death and long-term health complications including osteoporosis, depression, and reproductive complications.

• Increased communication with advertising agencies to encourage the use of age-appropriate, realistic models in ad campaigns and reduction of unrealistic computer enhancement in preteen and adolescent advertising campaigns.

- An overall ban of the use of photographic manipulation techniques that artificially slim images of fashion models throughout the entire fashion industry.

- Inclusion of models of varying weights and body types on both the catwalk and in fashion magazines so that these images—and the message that women and men of differing body types can look good in a variety of fashions—become part of our collective view of what constitutes beauty.

- Promotion of awareness in students, models, and the general public about advertising industry tactics, such as computer enhancement, used to falsify the appearance and actual size of models used in advertising.

- Collaboration with politicians, stakeholders, and eating disorder organizations to develop ethical self-regulatory codes for the fashion industry.

- Collaboration with politicians, stakeholders, and eating disorder organizations in widening the availability and affordability of effective eating disorders treatment, which must be made readily available to people in the fashion industry.

"If a designer envisions her creations being worn on a certain shape of body, that's her prerogative."

Banning Extremely Thin Models from Fashion Shows Is Problematic

Lindsay Beyerstein

Lindsay Beyerstein is a New York City–based writer. In the following viewpoint, Beyerstein presents a mixed view on Spain's 2006 ban on underweight models from fashion shows and its implications. She states that such regulation in the United States would censor a designer's right to free speech and present a creative aesthetic. Additionally, the author continues that weight minimums are arbitrary and do not evaluate models' health on an individual basis. Beyerstein, however, suggests that the fashion industry reject the emaciated look for the benefit of the modeling profession.

As you read, consider the following questions:

1. How does Lindsay Beyerstein define fashion?

Lindsay Beyerstein, "Emaciated Models and Occupational Health," *Majikthise*, October 2, 2006. Reproduced by permission. http://majikthise.typepad.com.

2. Why may weight requirements in modeling not fit within occupational health and safety regulation, in the author's opinion?

3. According to the author, what is objectionable about banning a model with an eating disorder from working?

L ately, there's been a lot of discussion in the feminist blogo-sphere about a new Spanish ban on emaciated models at the Cibeles fashion show:

> In accordance with the new regulations for this year's [2006] Cibeles fashion show 30% of models who appeared on its catwalk last year have been excluded for being too thin.

> The models have been rejected because they do not comply with new rules put into place by Madrid's Regional Government demanding that models present a healthy image with a [body mass index (BMI) of at least 18], i.e. they must weigh at least 56 kilos if their height is 1.75[m2]. These figures are approximately what the World Health Organization (WHO) considers to be the minimum healthy weight.

> The designer Jesus del Pozo made the announcement in a press conference during which Concha Guerra, Madrid's vice-director of Economy and Innovative Technology, laid out the new guidelines for the fashion show, which starts on 18th September [2007]. She said they had taken this unprecedented step because they were aware of the influence the popular Cibeles catwalk had on young girls' perception of fashion and ideal bodies. She explained that the Madrid government [was] aiming for healthier-looking models and getting away from the wasting-away appearance of many models, which was heavily criticised during the last Cibeles catwalk.

As a pro-labor feminist and a civil libertarian, I have mixed feelings about the Madrid rule.

The policy is clearly an infringement on the free speech of fashion designers. Design is a form of expression and a fashion show is an aesthetic undertaking. Designing clothes for aesthetic effect is a creative undertaking. If a designer envisions her creations being worn on a certain shape of body, that's her prerogative. Even if we think her aesthetics are indecent or her politics are blinkered and decadent, we should respect her right to realize her creative goal.

Putting on a fashion show is like staging a play or filming a movie. The whole production is engineered to create a particular aesthetic effect for the designer and the collection. A fashion show is also a live action ad, which makes it commercial speech.

The Madrid Regional Government's rationale for the new law is very troubling. Their main argument is that fashion shows should be regulated because they present an unhealthy ideal of beauty to the public and therefore constitute a public health risk. I have no doubt this is true, but I don't want the government to suppress ideas just because the larger society considers those ideas to be destructive. I certainly wouldn't want the *US* government taking any greater liberties on the censorship front.

An Occupational Health Risk

However, Amanda [Marcotte] raises a compelling counterargument at Pandagon [blog]. As she notes, the industry standard in modeling is an occupational health risk. A designer's right to design clothes for emaciated models doesn't necessarily guarantee her right to hire actual people to wear these clothes under dangerous conditions.

The average fashion model has a BMI of 16, which is well below what most medical experts consider a normal weight for a well-nourished adult. Only a fraction of post-pubescent women have a BMI below 18 for any reason.

Even for 15-year-old girls, a BMI of 16 is at the 3rd percentile. (That is, only 3% of American 15-year-olds are at or below the average weight of a fashion model.)...

Of course, models are hired precisely because they are physically atypical. Still, it's probably a myth that there are large numbers of people who are naturally thin enough to be catwalk models.

Of the women who currently have BMIs of 16 who are of modeling age, a large percentage are probably suffering from anorexia, substance abuse, and/or other health problems. It has been estimated that 1 percent of all American women suffer from full-blown anorexia nervosa. If less than 1 percent of 18-year-olds have a BMI of 16 for any reason, then 1 percent of 18-year-olds are anorexic. There must be considerable overlap because an extremely low weight is a necessary diagnostic criterion for anorexia nervosa. A person won't be diagnosed as anorexic unless [he or she is] lighter than the vast majority of people [his or her] height.

The fact that the current modeling industry standard is unhealthy for most aspiring models also contributes to an unhealthy professional culture in which even the thinnest models can become obsessive and paranoid about their weight. After all, one of the hallmarks of anorexia is the conviction that one is too fat despite being extremely thin.

The evidence is overwhelming that the current industry standards for fashion models are unhealthy for the vast majority of models. Professional pressure can contribute to the development of anorexia, the psychiatric condition with the highest mortality rate. Simply staying thin enough to be employable as a model can pose health risks, even in people who don't have anorexia. These include decreased bone density, infertility, slowed heartbeat, and in rare cases, death. I don't know if anyone has quantified the risks of long-term professional starvation and compared them to other occupational risks that we regulate. Aggressively dieting to stay 30 pounds underweight for a year probably is at least as unhealthy as working in a bar with second-hand smoke for the same period of time.

The Average Supermodel

Critics complain that models set an unattainable image for average women. When have supermodels ever looked like the average woman? Even in the '80s when models were more voluptuous, they never looked "average." How many Christie Brinkleys or Cindy Crawfords did you see at the mall or supermarket? Even if models weren't thin, they still had long legs, shiny hair and luminous skin for women to fawn over.

Katherine McGehee,
"Ban on 'Skeletal' Models Does Not Fix
Society's Obsession with Thinness,"
University Echo Online, *February 8, 2007.*

Not for the United States

If the current industry standard is dangerous for a lot of the people who work in the industry, it makes sense to submit the industry to some kind of regulation. However, the Madrid model would not be appropriate for the United States.

Restricting the aesthetics of fashion shows is an infringement of First Amendment rights. Don't tell me that fashion show free speech is trivial. I won't argue too strenuously that fashion shows make an important contribution to public discourse, but censorship is censorship. The only question is whether the benefit to the workers is sufficient to offset this infringement.

It is also difficult to see how a BMI restriction could fit into the existing legal framework for occupational health and safety regulation. The BMI standard looks at workers' bodies, not at their working conditions. So, the law affects people even if they are not putting themselves at risk in order to achieve a particular look. The health risks of having a BMI=n aren't the same for everyone. Some people can achieve the magic number with zero health risk, or minimal risk, while others can't even get close with life-threatening measures.

The issue is not how many people there are who are naturally and safely thin enough to be fashion models today. The BMI standard is arbitrary and that arbitrariness is problematic. You can't just deprive people of their livelihood because you want to send a larger message to an industry.

Furthermore, if anorexia is a work-induced disease, it seems perverse (and possibly illegal) to make women who suffer from the disease unemployable. It would set a very bad precedent to start making people unemployable because of medical/psychiatric conditions that don't affect their ability to do their job.

A Never-Ending Cycle

The best argument for minimum BMI laws is to rid the modeling community of the ruinous pressure to be ultra-thin. It's not that everyone who is that thin is at risk, it's that the current industry standards require most would-be models to put themselves at risk in order to be competitive. A BMI of 18 is still very thin by "civilian" standards. (The difference between BMIs of 16 and 18 amounts to about 10 lbs on a 5'9" model.) So, it's not as if the designers are being asked to sacrifice the slender aesthetic for the sake of public health.

The problem is that the current standards create a never-ending cycle of competition to be thinner. If we could somehow step back and say, okay, thin's fine but we shouldn't allow emaciated models to set the industry standard. All models would be better off if an outside force imposed a reasonable minimum weight for the whole profession. However, I don't see how such a rule could be legally imposed.

Periodical Bibliography

The following articles have been selected to supplement the diverse views presented in this chapter.

Laura Bond	"Ban on 'Skeletal' Models Does Not Fix Society's Obsession with Thinness," *The University Echo Online*, February 8, 2007.
Kevin M. Burke	"Design Piracy Prohibition Act—Finding the Middle Ground," *Apparel*, February 27, 2008.
Cleo Glyde	"Failure to Lunch," *Marie Claire*, April 2007.
Kerry Howley	"Couture Revolution: How Cheap Chinese Textiles Could Transform High Fashion," *Reason*, May 9, 2005.
Jeff Koyen	"Steal This Look—Will a Wave of Piracy Lawsuits Bring Down Forever 21?" *Radar*, February 22, 2008.
E.J. Mundell	"Furor over Anorexic Models Hits U.S. Fashion Week," *Washington Post*, February 2, 2007.
James Surowiecki	"The Piracy Paradox," *New Yorker*, September 24, 2007.
Juliette Terzieff	"Fashion World Says Too Thin Is Too Hazardous," Women's eNews, September 24, 2006.
Emili Vesilind	"UNDER THE LABEL—The New Pirates—Who Owns a Shape, a Cut, a Style? A Bill That Would Protect Designs Has the Fashion Industry Taking Sides," *Los Angeles Times*, November 11, 2007.
Marilyn Wann	"Self-Hatred and Celery Sticks," *Guardian*, November 21, 2008.
Eric Wilson	"Fashion Industry Grapples with Designer Knockoffs," *International Herald Tribune*, September 4, 2007.

OPPOSING
VIEWPOINTS®
SERIES

CHAPTER 4

What Is the Future of the Fashion Industry?

Chapter Preface

If Calvin Klein, Versace, and Oscar de la Renta are household names, then who are Comme des Garçons, Viktor & Rolf, and Gareth Pugh? Each is praised by the fashion press, name-checked by fashionistas, and worn by A-list clientele, after all. But Comme des Garçons, the Japanese label spearheaded by the reclusive Rei Kawakubo, expanded the vocabulary of fashion in the 1980s with destroyed fabrics, deconstructed garments, and black-on-black severity. Dutchmen Viktor Horsting and Rolf Snoeren, renowned for their visual witticisms and fine tailoring, had sent models rigged with glaring stage lights and blaring speakers down the runway. And Gareth Pugh, the English wunderkind who once shared a studio with squatters, exploded on the scene in 2006 with an extreme club-kid aesthetic and couture-like execution.

These designers are among the most celebrated avant-gardists in fashion. Their conceptual, subversive designs, however, often lack salability, mass appeal, or practicality. "It's fair to say thinkable fashions—yin to wearable's yang—have taken a bit of a backseat in recent years. . . ." suggests fashion editor Miles Socha. "Yet," he continues, "provocative and thought-provoking ideas remain a vital part of the fashion landscape: influencing and inspiring other designers, stimulating and engaging professionals, and sparking the change that is the engine of the industry. . . ."[1] For example, both Comme des Garçons and Viktor & Rolf have collaborated with fast-fashion giant H&M, creating edgy basics and accessories that sold out in a matter of hours. As for Gareth Pugh, R&B star Beyoncé unexpectedly traded her curve-hugging gowns for modified versions of his armor-like showpieces for a live performance and music video, bringing his outlandish, singular vision further into the mainstream."

Avant-garde designers are no less prone to faux pas than their conventional counterparts, and their creations have failed to appease many a fashion critic. Still, their forward-looking collections challenge the status quo and offer possible glimpses to the designs of tomorrow. In the following chapter, the authors forecast what lies ahead—and what is at stake—in fashion's future.

Notes

1. *WWD*, March 24, 2008.

▌ *"Couture is the key for . . . fashion."*

Haute Couture Fashion Is Thriving

Larry Elliott

Haute couture, or "high dressmaking," is the creation of one-of-a-kind garments using lavish fabrics and painstaking, often hand-executed techniques that meet rigorous standards. In the following viewpoint, Larry Elliott asserts that despite the recent economic downturn, haute couture is a bustling segment of the fashion industry. Though a single ball gown costs upward of $100,000, requires hundreds of hours of labor, and may not turn a profit, couture remains in demand, the author contends. Its clientele are the richest in the world, he states, and elite design houses embrace couture to enhance the cachet and allure of their brands. Elliott is the economics editor of the British newspaper Guardian.

As you read, consider the following questions:

1. In Elliott's opinion, how does couture "break" the rules of economics?

2. What two factors does Elliott claim have protected couture from decline?

3. How have luxury brands attempted to broaden their appeal, in the author's view?

As if paying homage to the all-pervasive mood of impending economic meltdown, the models strutting down the catwalk in their teetering heels, tight skirts and Greta Garbo-style bonnets would have looked at home in a glamorous Hollywood movie of the 1930s. John Galliano, creative supremo at Dior, it appeared, had heard that the International Monetary Fund [IMF] and George Soros are calling the yearlong credit crunch the biggest financial shock to the global economy since the 1930s and come up with a haute couture response: Depression chic.

Quite wrong, of course, and not just because this is not yet a 1930s style slump or anything like it. Any echoes of a bygone age are less to do with conjuring up memories of dole queues and soup kitchens than creating an impression of sumptuous glamour for a clientele so loaded that they are oblivious to the downturn.

A World Apart

Haute couture, quite simply, is a world apart. When asked for her views about the Armani collection, the young woman in the front row turned out to be a member of the Thai royal family. Her Royal Highness Princess Sirivannavari, 21, said she liked to come to the shows in Paris and Milan with an eye to buying couture shoes and bags, or perhaps an Armani jacket. "But I'm not the sort of person who shops all the time," she added. That may well be true, but to be frank, she did not appear to be the sort of person losing sleep over the global food crisis either.

At the same show, Dame Helen Mirren said she had been a fan of Armani since the 1980s. "The first time I got a good review about what I was wearing in a film was when I was wearing Armani in *The Comfort of Strangers*. I loved the jackets," she said of this season's show. "He always designs very wearable clothes." But would she buy a haute couture creation herself? "No, I can't afford it. It's so expensive."

A Bespoke Service

On the face of it, haute couture—one-off, hand-made creations—should be one of the first casualties of the credit crunch. The biggest housing bubble in America's history has gone pop, with the result that the parallel and linked bubble in the financial markets has also gone pop. Times for most of us are tougher than they were a year ago: food costs more; fuel costs more; mortgages are hard to find and expensive. As usual after years of excess, there is the unmistakable sense of belts being tightened.

In fact, haute couture is not just alive and well, but thriving. There is not the slightest scrap of evidence that the clientele in Paris have decided that the US sub-prime mortgage crisis means that this is the time to hunker down for a period of austerity. Life is sweet for the fashion houses where a made-to-measure ball gown can comfortably cost £50,000 and up to three times as much if the dress requires extensive embroidery.

In Paris this week [July 2008], the great names of the business—Chanel, Dior, Valentino, Givenchy—have been displaying their creations for the coming season. The clothes are fabulous and fabulously expensive, but a business model that seems to break every rule of modern economies seems to work. The idea is not to pile 'em high and sell 'em cheap, nor to outsource production to a sweatshop in India or China to ensure a fat profit margin, but to offer a bespoke service to women who want a work of art pieced together by hand over hundreds, even thousands, of hours in a workshop in Paris or Rome.

Stefano Sassi, chief executive of Valentino, flew in his needlewomen from Rome so that they could put the finishing touches to the collection. On the eve of the show, the firm's office overlooking the Place Vendôme was alive with last minute alterations and adjustments as the models tried on the outfits they would wear. Sassi said the effort was worth it. "Haute couture is exclusivity, beauty, a one-to-one relationship, luxury. It's timeless. There's always going to be a space for that kind of product. Rich people can recognise something that is unique.

"We are not worried about making money out of haute couture," he said. "It is the core of our image. We are talking about the essence of the brand. If we can make money, even better, but it is not the priority."

Even so, they don't exactly give the stuff away. The fashion equivalent of a Monet or a Degas costs money—big money—partly because the labour costs are stratospherically high and partly because the high price tag adds to the social cachet. This is the sort of world where if you need to know the price, it's definitely too expensive.

Marco Gobbetti, CEO of Givenchy, said: "For the moment, there don't seem to be any consequences of the economic situation on couture. The clients who are purchasing couture are not subject to this type of environment. Growth has been very strong over the past three seasons. It's not a dying business."

Business Sense

From the 1960s to the 1990s, there was a sense that couture was in gentle decline, confined to grandes Parisiennes of a certain age.

The high production costs and the small number of sales meant the profits on custom-made garments were much lower than on the mass market, but still pricey, prêt-à-porter ranges. This, though, failed to recognise two important factors—the

The Worst Place to Be in Fashion

Right now, the worst place to be in the fashion business is in the middle. Haute couture remains as haughty as ever, but chains at the lower end of the market like Zara and H&M have partially usurped the spots once occupied by moderately priced stores trading more on value-for-money than trendiness. And the upstarts' sprightly styles, often pinched from the designer labels, are forcing the big brands to rely on craftsmanship and the most extravagant materials to grab their customers' attention.

Marion Hume, "If You've Got It, Flaunt It,"
TIME, *March 6, 2005.*

determination of France to protect a tradition that it sees as just as integral to its national culture as haute cuisine or fine wine-making, and the arrival of the new, younger customer base.

Bruno Pavlovsky, chief executive of Chanel, said: "Couture is the key for Chanel and for fashion." Partly, he added, it is about keeping alive know-how, the traditional skills of dressmaking that have been lost as production has become mechanised and cheaper to serve a mass market. Chanel's one-off clothes are still made above Coco Chanel's old apartment in Paris's Rue Cambon. As a model of production, it is more William Morris than Primark, although what the old socialist would have made of old crafts being kept alive solely by demand from the super-rich is a moot point.

But for Chanel, it makes business sense. Pavlovsky said the 63 outfits shown at Tuesday's show might lead to 200 orders. The company, which sees its privately owned status as a bulwark against the short-termism of the stock market, is happy to send a team to Los Angeles or Moscow if that is what a customer wants. "It's the driver for the image."

At one level, this is just a posh way of saying that haute couture is a loss leader—a way for Chanel and Dior to boost their bottom lines by shifting industrial-style quantities of perfume and lipstick to the masses. Gobbetti, Pavlovsky and Sassi insisted, though, that there is more to it than that. Givenchy, Gobbetti said, uses haute couture in the way that a car company might use its research and development arm—as a place where the designers can be allowed to experiment without worrying about costs.

What companies are looking for from their couture ranges is brand identity that they can use to sell products to the mass market. The long boom in the west over the past 15 years has vastly increased the size of this market and for a conglomerate such as LVMH—which owns Dior—it is where the serious money is made.

It is the risk of serious retrenchment in this part of the business, rather than the niche couture market, that is starting to worry those at the top end of the fashion industry. The risk is that the Wall Street and City bankers being laid off or having their bonuses cut will be less inclined to splash out on a bag, or a bottle of scent. Tellingly, as Galliano was taking his bow at the end of Monday's show, the company was celebrating a £30m [million] legal victory over the online auctioneer eBay for its failure to stop sales of fake bags, lipsticks and designer clothes.

Tim Jackson, principal lecturer at the London School of Fashion, says that the last big shock to luxury brands came after 9/11 [September 11, 2001 terrorist attacks], because people stopped travelling, and a large proportion of luxury goods are bought by the well-off on their travels. There was, he says, a deliberate attempt to broaden the appeal of brands, with the sale of bags, jewellery and shoes that, while still expensive, were more affordable. "These goods have no issues with what's fashionable or size, and the goods have a high mark-up. There is a huge increase in directly operated stores, but they need high turnover to pay the overheads on the stores." Jackson says it will be this bit of the market—not the more exclusive haute couture niche—that will be affected by the credit crunch. The layoffs in the financial sector, falling property prices and higher inflation are all likely to have an impact.

In Paris earlier, Sassi made the same point. "The issue is not the super-rich, some of whom are doing well out of the crisis, but the people below the super-rich. Haute couture will last forever. It will only die when there are no ladies who are interested in beauty or feeling unique, or exclusivity."

The Rich Keep Getting Richer

While this helps explain the durability of haute couture, it doesn't quite explain why business has been so good in recent years. There are, however, solid economic reasons for the up-turn. One factor is that the rich keep getting richer, and there are more of them. The compression of incomes seen in the decades after the Second World War has been reversed; in Britain, for example, the gap between rich and poor has widened over the past decade, largely as a result of the salaries for the top 0.5% of earners.

Nick Tucker, market leader for the UK and Ireland at Merrill Lynch Global Wealth Management, said last week: "Spending by high net worth individuals [HNWIs] and ultra-high net worth individuals [UHNWIs] remains robust. The ongoing strength in both the global art market and luxury industries highlights that the wealthy will continue to spend despite clearly worsening economic conditions and explains why, historically, these industries weather global downturns."

According to a report by Merrill Lynch and Capgemini last month, there are now just over 10 million HNWIs in the world with a total wealth of $40 trillion. To qualify, you have to have net assets—excluding the value of your home—of

$4m. Qualifying as an UHNWI is tougher; there are 100,000 globally with net assets of $30m or more.

A second factor is that the new money has no hang-ups about ostentatious displays of conspicuous consumption. Prada announced this week that it was starting a made-to-order belt service for men and women, with a choice of patent leather, crocodile, saffiano or snakeskin, fastened with a buckle in antiquated silver or gold embellished with stones. Few doubted that there would be a market among those for whom money is no object.

Speaking after the Armani show, Susan Tabak, who is a consultant for those interested in buying couture, said: "If you want to be unique and have something to wear that nobody else has and can afford it, then why not? Why not have Monsieur Armani or John Galliano create something just for you? I think that's cool."

Finally, globalisation has meant that extreme wealth is no longer confined to western Europe and North America. The Thai princess rubs shoulders in the front row not just with the Oscar-winning film star but with the wife and daughter of the Russian oligarch making a killing out of the spiraling oil price. We may all, in other words, be paying an extra £20 a week to fill up our cars with petrol, but at least we are keeping the offspring of energy tsars in posh frocks. If it's any consolation (and it probably isn't), the frocks are totally gorgeous.

> *"The haute couture, once thought the grand dame of fashion, is anything but."*

Haute Couture Fashion Is Declining

Bridget Foley

Haute couture refers to the highest level of dressmaking and tailoring recognized in the fashion industry. In the following viewpoint, Bridget Foley declares that the ratified business and tradition of couture is in trouble. The labor-intensive, elaborate, and inaccessibly expensive designs are not moneymakers, Foley claims, and the roster of fashion houses that present couture collections has dwindled over the years. To boot, she insists that today's most influential designers offer ready-to-wear creations that are both more approachable and possess the fantastical qualities of couture. Foley is a contributor to Women's Wear Daily (WWD).

As you read, consider the following questions:

1. How has the clientele for couture changed, in the author's view?

2. What has happened to "Couture Week," according to Bridget Foley?

3. In Foley's opinion, why will the decline of couture have a negative impact on ready-to-wear designers?

Don't be fooled by the vivid flash of red, or the way Christian Lacroix's fanciful gown swishes so festively across the page. Such visual vibrancy aside, the haute couture, once thought the grand dame of fashion, is anything but. Rather, after generations of near-sacred status, fashion's most lauded fixture seems finally to be breathing her last. And, as with the passing of many a dowager who outlives most of her admirers, no one seems to notice much, not even in France, where fashion is revered as a national institution.

In truth, most of the real world has never felt the swell of such passion for couture. Now clients can still be found, often secretive Eastern types or emerging-economy divas who tread the tacky side of chic. But the list of well-known clients like those whose photos once telegraphed couture to the world has dwindled to nearly nil, and not for dearth of money. Hedge fund wives simply have not embraced the milieu as did their Nouvelle Society counterparts of a generation ago, while today's high-profile socials tend to be big-event borrowers rather than buyers.

A Money Loser

From the house standpoint, couture has long been a money loser, the loss traditionally offset by marketing value. Today, however, that whole premise is being re-evaluated, as not enough goes on in the arena to create excitement. "Couture Week" has slimmed down to a mere three days, the likes of Yves Saint Laurent, Emanuel Ungaro, Versace and Balmain long gone from the calendar. True, some of the major Place Vendôme jewelers have gotten clever, opening their high jewelry collections during the haute season. In fact, Chanel with its pearl collection, Van Cleef & Arpels with its tour-of-Paris motif and Boucheron with a magnificent, dark garden party stole the show from the couturiers. Even Louis Vuitton staged an event, showing a less trendy take on the Vuitton flower. As for the couture itself, Karl Lagerfeld and John Galliano are just as likely to leave their audiences breathless with delight, though this time the two anchors of the genre, Chanel and Dior, had disappointing efforts. For fall [2006], they went very separate ways, Lagerfeld focusing on thigh-high denim boots for a faux girl-of-the-people look, while Galliano took inspiration from the devil himself, or at least a film based on a fable about the devil, the results looking angry indeed, and none too pretty.

Jean Paul Gaultier also turned to fable: Jean Cocteau's *Beauty and the Beast*. Its irresistible counterpoints—male and female, good and evil, light and dark—made the perfect setup for lavish reworkings of the designer's classics: intricate knits, confident pantsuits and a shiny python trench coat trimmed in silver fox. For his Prive, Giorgio Armani showed lovely romantic gowns by night and clothes that seemed targeted to the Russian arriviste set by day.

Lacroix proved the star of the season in a dazzler that swayed from storybook fantasy to considerable restraint. To open, he took two ordinary wardrobe items, trench coat and parka, and elevated them to elitist perfection, the former a huge triangle tiered in back; the latter, a lavish fur-laden brocade over a simple dress. This combination proved to be an important theme, as time and again, a model would slip off her elaborate coat—bands of fox and lace; fox-trimmed silver leaf on felt—to reveal a short, flirty dress. The week's other star was Valentino. His smart, alluring collection was of the kind that garnered him the Légion d'Honneur, which he accepted from the minister of culture with a short, emotional speech. "I have remained very faithful to France," the Italian native said.

No New Blood

Such niceties aside, once, virtually all of fashion's most directional participants were couturiers; today, that is true of only a handful, with no new blood in sight. An exception is

No Longer the Bread and Butter

Today the haute couture collection is no longer the bread and butter of the fashion industry and more and more houses have shied away from producing this expensive and niche line in favour of prêt-à-porter (or ready-to-wear) collections and, of course, accessories.

And, while Paris is still seen as a fashion capital, it is no longer the only capital. We have London, New York and Milan and many other contenders. So, the concept of Paris as the sole arbiter of high fashion no longer holds water.

"Haute Couture,"
February 12, 2008. www.canada.com.

Givenchy's Riccardo Tisci, who once again substituted deep-thoughts pretension for a fashion message. More to the point, couture is no longer the sole stage for fantastical creation. Now some of the best, most influential ready-to-wear designers show de facto couture along with their more approachable designs. Balenciaga's intricately crafted laces that Nicolas Ghesquiére offered last spring were made in the Lesage atelier now owned by Chanel and were shown in multiple layers that, when put together at retail, cost about $40,000. The runway epics of Domenico Dolce and Stefano Gabbana are designed with their own Dolce & Gabbana stores in mind; fall's embroidered Josephine gowns start at $60,000. (The designers open their more expansive wholesale collection to retailers in private showroom presentations.) Not even the most discreet of Viktor Horsting and Rolf Snoeren's silver-dipped heirlooms for Viktor & Rolf were intended to see a sales floor. And the awesome showpieces that Alexander McQueen mixes in with his ready-to-wear—for fall featuring a pheasant-feather dress and wildlife chapeaus—could hardly be considered off the rack.

Still, all of the above technically falls under the auspices of ready-to-wear, a realm now almost obsessed with the antithesis of couture, those uber merchy preseasons. So guess what has muscled in on the week once dedicated to that most elitist fashion? Several years ago, Lanvin's Alber Elbaz took to showing his prespring collection to editors during the couture. Since then, others have joined in, including designers presiding over tiny houses, such as Azzaro's Vanessa Seward. Still others take the opportunity to show full spring. Among them: Anne Valerie Hash, who has quietly become an impressive seller at edgy outposts such as London's Dover Street Market.

Which is not to say the demise of couture will impact the industry's little guys positively—anything but. High-end fashion, ready-to-wear included, is an immensely expensive proposition, not only to buy and wear, but also to produce and sell, and not all deep-pocketed organizations are willing to ante up. During Couture Week, Rochas's Olivier Theyskens, one of fashion's most talented and talked-about young stars, left retailers and editors gleeful with a spectacular prespring collection. Soon after, *Women's Wear Daily*, *W*'s sister publication, broke the news that Rochas's parent company, Procter & Gamble, which took control of the house when it acquired Wella several years ago, will discontinue ready-to-wear operations as soon as it can wind its way through the labyrinth of French labor laws. Potential backers are no doubt already lining up. But coupled with the couture malaise, the episode suggests that in this world of ever-escalating prices, the sky may no longer be the limit.

> "Green fashion has definitely expanded
> outward from its 'hippie' connotations
> of the past."

Green Fashion Is the Future
of the Fashion Industry

Brita Belli

Brita Belli is managing editor of E/The Environmental Magazine. *In the following viewpoint, Belli writes that green fashion,
which uses environmentally friendly textiles and repurposed materials, is expanding. Forward-thinking eco-designers, she states,
are creating sustainable, cutting-edge lines that offer alternatives
to cheap and expendable mass-produced styles. While sustainability has trickled into the mainstream through famous brand
names and major retailers, Belli says that consumer demand for
green fashion is not yet great enough to make over the industry.
The author proposes that this niche market will continue to
grow and larger corporate initiatives will help create lasting
change.*

As you read, consider the following questions:

1. Why is sourcing fabrics and materials difficult for
   emerging green designers, in the author's opinion?

2. In Brita Belli's view, how does buying green fashion influence consumers?

3. How has consumer demand for organic cotton changed, as stated by the author?

Today's eco-designers don't talk about being inspired by leaves falling or icecaps melting; they're starry-eyed for futuristic-looking chairs, towering skyscrapers and folding bicycles. They're thinking like architects, leading with design and textile as opposed to an activist agenda.

"The way a chair breaks up space or a building cuts into the sky with so many different views is how I feel a garment relates to the body," says Brooklyn designer Nina Valenti, who launched the sustainable line NatureVsFuture in 2002. "I design pieces that have a strong line, form and texture." Her clothing has severe pleats and soft gathers, military stiffness and feminine slits, the yin and yang of organic and technological forces. Her fabrics range from the expected organic cottons, wools, hemps and soys to fabrics made from recycled soda bottles.

Form and Function

A folding bicycle provided the inspiration for Los Angeles designer Carol Young's spring collection. Specifically, it was the Dahon folding bicycle made by a company founded to encourage environmentally sustainable forms of transport. "What I loved about the Dahon Ciao," says Young, "was not just its functionality, but its aesthetics, individuality and its 'morphability.'"

Young's label, undesigned, is a study in wearable sustainable fashion that is decidedly modern in its ability to transcend season and move between office, bicycle, subway and sidewalk. There are skinny jeans layered with dotted, form-fitting dresses topped with demure shrugs. Bold pockets and soft hoodies and bubbled edges. "Rather than sketching traditional fashion figures, I prefer making paper models, and then samples to 'test drive' in the real world," Young says. "Clothing design is in a sense architecture miniaturized, made on a more intimate level. Both are experiential, functional design; both transform 2-D to 3-D and are shaped by the materials they're made from. The way that the green movement is changing the building industry is similar to how it's shaping the apparel industry."

As a former architecture student and an avid cyclist, Young gives recycled clothing and organic fabrics new life as fashionable dresses, skirts, jackets and pants that stretch and move according to the needs of the "urban nomad." These are people who live in cities—Paris, New York, London, San Francisco— who use mass transit, and who need clothing that's flexible enough to take them from day to night. She mentions, among this clientele, "artistic/eclectic professionals" as well as "academics, architects, curators, graphic designers and filmmakers." She does not mention hippies among the lot.

In fact, in undesigned's shape-hugging black, white and gray pieces, there is nothing that might be paired with Birkenstocks and a Mexican poncho. More and more, sustainable clothing reflects the future not the past. Online, it is serious connoisseurs of art, architecture and fashion who follow the movements of sustainable design, debating similarities between scrap wood coffee tables on Inhabitat.com or the ethics of using recycled leather in shoes on FiftyRX3.blogspot.com. And then there are the dedicated crafters who detail how to knit shopping totes from cut-up plastic bags or weave purses from old seatbelts.

Refashion has taken the idea of vintage to a new level. Mass-produced clothing is uniformly cheap and trendy, and each season another line of expendable merchandise joins the landfill heaps. But extending the life cycle of clothing has progressed beyond bedazzling the back pockets of a pair of Levi's. From amateur how-to sites like Ohmystars.net teaching "T-shirt surgery" to one-of-a-kind silk-screened bamboo tank tops on craft site Etsy.com to boutiques like Hairy Mary's on New York's Lower East Side selling reconstructed vintage dresses, refashioning is pushing the idea that each item of clothing tells a story.

Admitted "fashion nerd and art freak" Jill Danyelle started the blog FiftyRX3 to document a personal project, but evolved the site into a place to discuss emerging green designers.

"Green fashion has definitely expanded outward from its 'hippie' connotations of the past," says Danyelle, who is also the fashion editor for inhabitat.com. "We have seen expansion all the way into high-end designer looks down to Wal-Mart. This is what I see as true growth. Yet the percentage of the marketplace is still so miniscule that I believe eco-friendly design in the fashion industry is far from established."

Ethics and Anti-Fashion

While many eco-designers seem engaged in their own personal *Project Runway* competition—finding stylish ways to rework vintage neckties and discarded tires—others have come to this new fashion frontier led by ethical concerns first. Irish label Edun ("nude" spelled backwards), founded by U2 singer Bono and wife Ali Hewson in conjunction with New York designer Rogan Gregory, is up-front about its mission. The designers want their customers to think about the cotton in their clothing and how it was produced. Behind Edun's image of pale, punk-looking models in pricey tees and skinny jeans is the motto "trade not aid," a focus on raising Africa's share of the global cotton market.

African cotton farmers are "using expired pesticides and . . . are subject to grave negative health effects," says Bridget Russo, an Edun spokesperson. These farmers "often make a loss every year," she says, "and some . . . sleep 10 to 20 people in a hut with one pair of shoes among them all."

The company notes on its Web site that if the fashion industry would increase its trade with Africa by one percent, it would provide the country an additional $70 million in exports, which is "several times more than what the region currently receives in international assistance."

While Edun is committed to using organic fabrics, the company puts sustainable trade first—improving the economic condition of third world farmers. It uses organic materials whenever possible. "At the moment, our T-shirts and fleece items are 100 percent organic cotton," says Russo, "which makes up 50 percent of the overall collection."

UK designer Katharine Hamnett laid the groundwork for anti-fashion-fashion back in the 1980s with her bold black-on-white message shirts (like the anti-drug "Choose Life" T-shirt seen on George Michael in a Wham! video). Hamnett's latest T-shirt reads "Save the Future," and it's a line she produced in partnership with the Environmental Justice Foundation [EJF] for its campaign to end child labor in cotton farming, especially in Uzbekistan.

In the 1990s, most industry insiders didn't share Hamnett's outrage over laborers dying from pesticide exposure, and she was dismissed by many of her peers. So she cut ties with her Italian manufacturer and tried to produce her own ethical line at a time when organic cotton was nearly impossible to find. Now, in 2007, a Wal-Mart-like UK retailer named Tesco carries Hamnett's sustainable clothes and the designer who couldn't find a friend in fashion is in the swirling center of the eco-fashion popularity club.

The Search for Sustainable Fabrics

Major labels can order large quantities of organic cotton for a mainstream clothing line, but emerging eco-designers face a series of challenges. Most mills aren't interested in producing specialty fabrics in small quantities, forcing designers to use an extremely limited color palette (those olive greens, burlap

What's Hot Right Now: Bamboo

In terms of popularity, bamboo clothing is what's hot right now. Bamboo, a type of grass, is one of the fastest growing, renewable resources on the planet. As a fabric, it has a natural ability to breathe and keeps you cooler in summer and warmer in winter, according to Fashionandearth.com. It has a silk-like softness and is much more absorbent and naturally more wrinkle-resistant than cotton.

Lashonda Stinson Curry, "Eco-Chic,"
The Gainesville Sun, *May 15, 2009.*

browns and dusty off-whites) or find creative alternatives from recycling fabrics to making one-of-a-kind pieces. At an airing of New York eco-design talent called Project Earth Day held at the spacious Teknion showroom in New York's SoHo district this past spring, a bright floral dress by Brooklyn designer Bahar Shahpar stood out in the sea of earth tones.

The fashion show was the first from the U.S. Green Building Council's Emerging Green Builders New York. Eco-design was showcased wherever possible, from the runway made of recycled milk jugs, soda bottles and laundry detergent containers to the recycled cardboard podium. Student designers competed for a $1,500 prize followed by a runway show from New York's eco-fashion establishment: Loyale, NatureVsFuture, Doie, Ryann.

Shahpar was the night's runway stylist, and the jumper dress she'd designed was luminous with color: red, blue and pink flowers spilled across the fabric as though caught mid-blossom.

"Without a doubt, the most difficult part of designing sustainably is the sourcing of fabrics and materials," Shahpar says. "Choice is extremely limited in terms of color and print—largely because most mills and suppliers have very high minimums (ranging from 200 to 1,000 yards) for customizing fabrics. . . . As consumer demand for sustainably produced clothing grows, we hope the manufacturers will be willing to broaden their range of stock fabrics and colors."

Another Brooklyn designer, Raina Blyer of the Ryann line, sticks to solid prints—shirts that wrap, or fall in soft gathers, creating feminine lines but allowing for movement. When it comes to finding organic fabric (she prefers hemp, soy and cotton blends), she says simple is the only option. "There are very limited options," Blyer says, "and only from a few sources. There's [also] a problem with consistency and color."

Until wider fabric varieties become available to fledgling designers, some like Young use designer surplus to add color and texture to their collections. Others reach out to friends and family for usable material. The designers behind the tattoo and rock n' roll-inspired T-shirts at New York's SDN use T-shirts as blank canvases and sell the silk-screened final products through eco-boutiques like Sodafine in Brooklyn and Kaight on Manhattan's Lower East Side. "We actively find old T-shirts and cold water dyes," says Kyle Goen who started the line with lifelong friend Marcus Hicks. "We put the word out to friends before they throw them out. We clean them, dye them and silkscreen them. It's tough to find T-shirts with nothing on them."

Designers want to distance themselves from the shapeless eco-fashions of yesteryear, when words like "hemp" and "organic" inspired visions of hippies in a hacky sack circle. While the colors are limited, the cut, the fit and the high-end price tags suggest sophistication. No one, it seems, wants to look eco. In fact, designers often take pride in the fact that the sustainability of their clothing is not immediately recognizable.

"Most of the people who shop at the studio boutique [in L.A.] come in for the design," says Young, "then are happy to hear about the fabrics."

Shahpar would rather not be boxed in by a green label. "I'm encouraged by the attention I receive as an 'eco-designer,'" she says, "but my hope is that my customer will pick up my clothing because they appreciate the design ... the story and the process that went into each piece."

Mainstream Bound

While eco-fashion has trickled into the mainstream via the organic Eco jeans line from Levi's, men's organic T-shirts from the Gap and American Apparel's Sustainable Edition organic line, consumer demand has not been loud enough to merit a major market turnover. It's the fashion-savvy who seem to think about the content of their clothes, while the majority of shoppers are influenced mostly by price—an arena where organics have trouble competing. In purchasing sustainable clothing, consumers are being asked to think about the big picture: how the jeans or T-shirts they buy might support a local organic cotton industry or better quality of life for farmers in Africa.

"I think we will continue to see a lot of this fractured environmentalism, where some people may be concerned with emissions and global warming, but not with toxins or water conservation," Danyelle says. "My mission became eco-friendly clothing because I found it my biggest challenge in living sustainably."

What's needed, according to designers like Young, is a shifting of consumer consciousness. Shoppers have become used to the disposable clothing model. But they could, instead, treat clothing as "something cherished." Young says, "I'd rather have a few things that I love than a closet full of things that I'll never wear and have no connection to."

Just as consumers once bought organic food before deciding to go one step further—buying locally grown—they might start to consider who grew their cotton and who turned it into a wearable object. "It's nice to have a person behind the product," Danyelle says.

Edun says it's already seeing a significant change in the way consumers approach shopping. But the company, like many eco-fashion lines, serves a higher-end clientele—customers more likely to shop at Nordstrom and Barneys than Target. "In the end, shopping is politics," says Russo.

Economic choices can have a significant impact on how clothing is produced. But even though demand for organic cotton clothing doubled between 2005 and 2006 according to the Organic Consumers Association (growing faster than organic food), it still represents a very small percentage of the market. Cotton Incorporated executive vice president Mark Messura says his organization has been tracking consumer interest for the past decade and most shoppers have little interest in organic cotton. "We did a comprehensive study with the Organic Trade Association," Messura says, "and most consumers don't understand organic, especially when it comes to clothing. Most don't put importance on environmentally friendly fabric." Instead, he says, shoppers are interested in color, style and price. As he says, "We don't eat clothing."

Instead, the most noticeable environmental changes in the clothing industry are coming from businesses wanting to extol their own corporate virtues. Gap, for example, has a representative on the Better Cotton Initiative (BCI) Steering Committee. BCI promotes environmentally, socially and economically sustainable cotton cultivation around the globe and aims to put "Better Cotton" into the supply chain by 2012. Other representatives who've joined BCI come from H&M, adidas and IKEA. When Gap's Banana Republic stores sold a hemp blend skirt or fragrances in certified sustainable wood boxes, they generated positive publicity from both environmental outlets and mainstream media.

Back in 1996, outdoor and adventure clothing specialist Patagonia switched its entire sportswear line to organically grown cotton. The company is a leader in following ethical practices. Messura calls Patagonia "very genuine and very honest" about its efforts.

Trendsetting, sustainably made designer fashions will continue to attract a growing niche market, but these larger corporate initiatives are the kind that can create lasting change in the marketplace. "I believe corporations need to take responsibility for how they produce their products," says Danyelle, who also advocates "government-regulated labeling" so consumers will know if the clothes they are purchasing meet their social and environmental standards. The more consumers know about the content of their clothing, the more they may begin to see it in all of its "life cycle," from grower to garment. The eco-fashion movement, on a small or large scale, is about drawing the connections between consumers and their clothing, moving away from a disposable mentality. It's a major shift for a generation accustomed to buying clothes with a shopping cart.

> "Without any certification or governing
> bodies overseeing the greening of the
> fashion industry, any label with any
> degree of eco-ambition can color itself,
> well, green."

Consumers Should Approach Green Fashion with Caution

Gloria Sin

In the following viewpoint, Gloria Sin suggests that some so-called "green fashion" lines do not live up to their environmentally friendly claims. Lacking oversight in the fashion industry, companies and retailers jumping on the eco-fashion bandwagon can label their designs as green even if sustainable processes or materials are not used, Sin alleges. Therefore, she advises shoppers to be aware of such marketing tactics, also known as "greenwashing," and that following green fashion is about conscientious consumer choice and influencing businesses to reduce their carbon footprints. Sin works at Mansueto Digital, a publishing company based in New York City.

As you read, consider the following questions:

1. What sets eco-friendly labels apart from the rest of the fashion industry, in Gloria Sin's view?

2. According to Sin, what challenges await green designers in the marketplace?

3. How does Terri Spaek-Merrick reduce waste and energy consumption in producing her fashion line, as stated by the author?

The zebra-like, black-and-white, elongated shrug keeps disappearing from the rack at the flagship Barneys New York store on Fifth Avenue in Manhattan. To customers, the incredibly soft and warmer-than-wool sweater is a must-have, even though most have no idea what the hangtag means by "Alpaca" or "Rogan."

Rogan is actually an avant-garde line by Rogan Gregory, whose various ventures—from denim to furniture—are businesses with an eco-friendly bent. The designer is best known for his high-end organic denim line Loomstate, and his collaboration with rock star Bono's Edun collection.

Made of fur from free-range Alpacas (multicolor, sheep-like llama cousins, native to Peru) handspun into yarn, Gregory's popular sweater is knit with naturally black and white yarn so no toxic dyes are used to achieve its two-tone look. With herders continuingly breeding out the non-white species due to underwhelming demand (white fleece is easier to dye and therefore more commercially viable), Gregory uses the sweater to bring awareness to this inhumane practice as part of his "Save Our Colored Brother" campaign.

This sweater, and not some burlap sac rescued from the trash can by granola-eating hippies, is the essence of green fashion. What sets eco-fashion apart from conventionally produced garments is the environmental, ethical and even social considerations weaved into the design of each piece. It can be as simple as using a sustainable fabric like organic cotton and donating proceeds to an earth-friendly charity, or as extensive as providing ethical employment to offshore factory workers. Across the entire fashion spectrum, from accessories to haute couture, designers are finding ways to incorporate their green lifestyles into their work.

Of course, not every brand is as considerate of its eco-impact as Rogan. Without any certification or governing bodies overseeing the greening of the fashion industry, any label with any degree of eco-ambition can color itself, well, green. This means companies that use recycled paper hangtags are on the same eco-platform as those running on wind power. For example, Banana Republic recently launched a 50-piece green collection. The pieces push all the right buttons—their 100 percent recycled paper price tags have names like "Bamboo Printed Wrap" and "Leaf Tee"—but as may often be the case, the actual clothing may not be made in an eco-friendly production process or even from sustainable materials. Besides, would the average shopper at the local mall even know the difference?

"It's a catch-22," says Alice Demirjian, director of Fashion Marketing at Parsons at The New School. "To be truly sustainable is to buy less." Designers are well aware they need to educate consumers to make a business out of sustainable fashion. Not only do they need to differentiate themselves from other green designers (especially from eco-posers), and spread the word about the virtues of greening the industry, they also need to compete with non-eco-products, which tend to be more reasonably priced. This is why marketing is key for these labels. But there is a difference between informing customers and outright fibbing about environmental claims, also known as greenwashing. According to many environmentalists and critics of this practice, marketers often employ tactics that paint products greener than they actually are.

As more and more mass retailers like Wal-Mart and the Gap jump on the green fashion bandwagon, they're looking to established indie labels for direction and inspiration. green-Karat jewelry, Olivia Luca couture, and Mink shoes may not be household names, but their success is proving to mainstream brands that going green is good for business.

greenKarat

Back in 2003 when he co-founded greenKarat, the ecologically and socially responsible jeweler and CEO, Matt White, didn't know a whole lot about jewelry-making. But as a CPA, he knew the numbers in the gold-mining industry didn't add up. "Two thousand five hundred tons of gold [are] mined each year, even though there is already enough idle gold above ground to satisfy the jewelry industry for the next 50 years," White says. This is why his company makes a point of using only recycled gold and other metals in made-to-order pieces. In fact, the myKarat recycling program provides store credit in exchange for gold jewelry for melting.

Likewise, baubles in greenKarat designs only reuse stones—or they make their own. Using heat and pressure to simulate the conditions under which Mother Nature produces diamonds and other rocks, created gems are as real as the naturals because they share the same chemical makeup. In White's opinion, lab-grown gems should eliminate the need for mining that harms both the environment and miners.

Though White has noticed an explosion of new green jewelers this year, he's concerned most of his competitors don't disclose their products' origins even though they're working under the same limitations. greenKarat customers get a detailed report tracing their purchase's history, including the not so eco-friendly parts. While brick-and-mortar stores are interested in carrying his work, he is wary of potential pitfalls. "There's a lot of greenwashing out there," he says. "By selling

"... so I decided to make us all fabulous new outfits from the Guardian environment supplement!"

"...so I decided to make us all fabulous new outfits from the Guardian supplement," cartoon by Clive Goddard. www.CartoonStock.com.

only through our Web site, at least I can control the message and try to educate consumers about their purchases."

Olivia Luca

"In the past two months, I've done the same amount of business as my first six," says eco-couture designer Terri Spaek-Merrick, whose online cut-sew-and-ship dressmaking business is barely a year-old. The veteran Portland designer, who maintains a physical bridal studio called Embellish, is expanding online to reach green-conscious customers who shop on the Web.

Her Olivia Luca Web site is essentially a digital game of dress up, where users can click on options from skin tone to eco-fabric before submitting the order. Not only does the designer promote the use of sustainable fabrics on the site, she also designed the concept right into her business. To minimize overhead costs and waste, she doesn't order any materials until she can confirm a design job. Pieces are produced in-house using couture technique, which means a lot of hand rather than machine sewing with a minimal carbon footprint. As a result, her custom-eco-formal wear prices are quite accessible, even for the average green conscious customer. An Olivia Luca custom gown might run a couple hundred dollars, while a Vera Wang Luxe Collection starts at $6,000—and the Luca is eco-chic and shipped directly to your home.

Mink

Unlike greenKarat or Olivia Luca, Mink isn't really a green fashion company. It is a high-end vegan footwear brand created by vegan stylist Rebecca Brough out of frustration that sexy yet animal-cruelty-free shoes didn't exist back in 2002. As it turns out, what's animal-friendly tends to be good for the environment.

Determined to create leather-free high heels that belong on the same shelf as Gucci and Prada, Brough spent one and a half years in Italy finding a willing shoemaker to give vegan shoes a try. From four-inch heel stilettos in scarlet to bold lines of sequins cascading over the foot, it's hard to remember the trendsetting products are earth-friendly. Not only are embellishments like sequins and buckles sourced from vintage surplus stores, some heels are made of recycled cork or wood, organic cotton fabrics instead of leather, and each shoe is handmade for minimal energy consumption, not to mention maximum comfort.

Department stores that just a few years ago wouldn't give her the time of day are actively approaching her to retail her shoes. While Brough still relies on styling gigs to finance her vegan shoe business, she knows that what she's doing is better for the environment. "This is the right thing to do, even if it means I won't get rich from it," she says.

Ultimately, going green in fashion isn't about riding on an imaginary train through clever marketing. For businesses, it's about recognizing the environmental costs involved in every decision and finding innovative ways to minimize that cost. For consumers, it's realizing the influence spending holds on businesses and leveraging that for positive change.

| "*Clothes sites appear to be back in fash-ion.*"

Online Fashion Retail Is Growing

Victoria Furness

In the following viewpoint, Victoria Furness claims that online fashion retail is heading toward significant growth. She says that convenience, twenty-four-hour shopping, and high-speed Internet access are the main drivers of the market. Also, Furness adds that more shoppers are logging on to find unique, hard-to-find items not found in brick-and-mortar stores. Online fashion retail and customer services are still developing, but she insists that re-tailers should not ignore the Internet's potential to increase sales and foster brand loyalty. Furness is a technology and business writer.

As you read, consider the following questions:

1. As stated by Victoria Furness, why did Boo.com fail?

2. According to Susanne Goller, what is lacking in the on-line shopping experience?

3. What is problematic in giving online shoppers a greater interactive experience, in Furness's view?

A s clothing retailers pour more cash online, Victoria Furness finds out if the market is set to really take off.

'Two years' work, five offices overseas, 350 staff. All these people trusted me and now I have failed them. What have I done? How could things have gone so wrong?' writes Ernst Malmsten, one of Boo.com's three founders, in *Boo Hoo: A Dot.com Story from Concept to Catastrophe*, his account of the soaring highs and plummeting lows that led to online fashion retailer Boo's demise.

Perhaps rather tragically, Boo.com was experiencing steady growth in sales—$500,000 (£274,000) in its final two weeks—yet this wasn't enough to stop it being overwhelmed by a catalogue of errors, which included technological incompatibilities, overambitious global expansion, over-inflated visitor expectations and a loose approach to company spending.

In the immediate aftermath of the dot-com bust, prospects for e-commerce were bleak, but particularly so for clothing. Yet, clothes sites appear to be back in fashion. According to Verdict Research, the online clothing market was worth £873 million in 2005, an increase of 24.5 percent on the previous year. And it forecasts £2.27 billion by 2010.

Although women are prolific online shoppers, more men are buying clothes on the Web, up from 30 percent in 2003 to 40 percent in 2005, according to Verdict.

Some of the biggest factors driving growth are also driving the e-commerce market as a whole: convenience, 24/7 shopping and high-speed Web access.

Statistics from Nielsen//NetRatings found that, in December 2003, 72.3 percent of the UK population had connection speeds of up to 128k. Now that figure is only 17.2 percent, as two-thirds enjoy 512k.

Unique Items

One unique driver behind the clothing market is the opportunity to buy items that are hard to find on the high street. This might be the reason why, in a recent survey by Verdict, eBay was the retailer most shoppers visit to buy clothing and footwear. 'eBay offers the opportunity to capture one-off pieces of clothing from all over the world,' says Harsha Wickremasinghe, retail analyst at Verdict Research.

Azita Qadri, small business manager at eBay and former manager of the clothing category, agrees this was initially why clothing sold well on the auction site. Since then, the category has grown at a tremendous rate. 'A piece of women's clothing sells every seven seconds on the UK site. People saw there was demand and started listing items they had worn once, as well as new clothes. Then young designers started using the site and small businesses wanting to sell excess stock,' she adds. It hopes to boost sales with the launch of eBay Express, a new site where small firms can sell new items at fixed prices.

Certainly, the clothing market is seeing greater investment from online retailers as well as traditional outlets and mail-order providers. Next, the most popular online clothing retailer, saw a 13.7 percent rise in sales in its Next Directory division (which includes online) in 2005, taking total revenue to £685m [million]. It attributed a significant proportion of this increase to growth in online purchases. ASOS, an online retailer targeting celebrity and fashion-conscious buyers, saw group revenue increase by 39 percent this year to reach £18.8m.

Meanwhile, several latecomers have launched new stores online, such as luxury brands Marni, Louis Vuitton and Kurt Geiger. The latter has already reported that sales from its site, which launched last October [2005], are double its expectations.

Shoppers' Brains Online

"While shoppers' brains screen out 99% of the visual stimuli they are presented with on the high street, it is only 45% when they shop online," explains [Envision Retail operations director] Jason Kemp.

"So there is a huge opportunity to provide even more pictures of products, from various angles, in close up, to get customers hooked—but getting them to that stage means that any previous searching and downloading has to be fast."

Because they can't touch the garment, fashion surfers need more imagination to assess a product's suitability.

"They physically move towards the screen to try and get a closer look; they stop to think while they imagine wearing the item and then check out descriptive words to understand the texture," explains Kemp.

just-style.com,
"Clothing Companies Cash in on E-Commerce,"
February 13, 2007.

Social Aspect

But, despite encouraging growth, Susanne Goller, director of the retail and leisure division at research agency Ipsos-MORI, says most fashion retailers' Web services haven't worked as well as hoped. 'Part of the reason is that fashion customers, who are primarily female, like the social aspect of shopping,' she explains. 'Online clothing retailers do not give the same experience. Often, clothes are presented in a boring way, the pictures are small, the outfits incomplete and you cannot home in on the fabric, so you don't know what you're buying.'

For this reason, many retailers that have had a Web site for several years are redesigning, rebuilding and relaunching them.

The common goal is to make their service more compelling and entice consumers to spend more.

Revamped sites such as Adams.co.uk, have brought more stock online, so visitors can buy items that are unavailable in their local store. 'We convinced Adams to bring about 600 different product lines online to make it quite a large category,' says Oliver Schonrock, CEO at e-commerce agency Real TSP, which developed the Adams Kids site.

When Topshop.com relaunches soon, it will feature every clothing line, with a few concessions. 'It will be representative of our Oxford Circus flagship store,' says TopShop brand director Jane Shepherdson.

Window Dressing

Clothing Web sites are also becoming more sophisticated, as retailers try to replicate the off-line experience. 'A whole profession has been built around shop window dressing and that hasn't been for nothing,' says Goller. 'But, with today's technologies there's no reason why you cannot make Web sites interesting.'

Sites such as Marksandspencer.com and Adams.co.uk, for example, make greater use of photography and professional styling. 'Marks & Spencer used to feature mannequins wearing its clothes, but we've changed this to include real people and close-up pictures of garments,' says Laurent Ezekiel, client services director at M&S's agency, Wheel, whose other clients include Laura Ashley and Ted Baker.

Designer retailer Net-a-Porter manages its photography in-house. 'Our aim is to get the consumer as close to the product as possible,' explains head of marketing Martin Bartle, who previously worked at Boo, [and] thinks the concept offered by Net-a-Porter, which combines editorial with retail, has helped it to double turnover since launch; last year [in 2005] it generated £21.5m. 'A high-fashion customer is looking for advice,' he says. 'If you're spending up to £800 on a handbag, you'll want to know why it's the 'it' bag of the moment.'

A more personalised shopping experience is a key trend in the sector, as retailers try to engender loyalty among shoppers. At present, Net-a-Porter customers can e-mail the site and seek advice on a garment's fit.

'The next step might be to have online stylists guide you in what to wear, not just how to wear it,' adds Bartle.

Indeed, many retailers seek to offer inspiration and advice to boost cross-selling. Net-a-Porter and Marks & Spencer's sites offer outfit suggestions when a visitor clicks on an item of clothing. 'The next step will be for sites to suggest products based on customer order histories and registered preferences, such as designers or styles,' says Neil McCarthy, commercial director at e-commerce agency Tamar.

H&M has tried to overcome the problem of not being able to try clothes on by offering a virtual 'dressing room'. Users create a model based on their size and click on items to find out what size they need. Women's retailer New Look has tried something similar. But, such efforts are overshadowed by limited stock and the lack of an e-commerce engine at both sites.

Usability Issues

While new technology is enabling retailers to offer a greater interactive experience, many are going back to basics. Top-Shop, for example, is eliminating Macromedia Flash from its site as it increases the time it takes to load pages. Accessibility is a big issue in online retail, where the focus tends to be on design. High-street retailer River Island was criticized this year for launching an entirely Flash-based site that is inaccessible to disabled users, and even the most popular sites still have issues with usability.

When mail-order provider Boden brought its site back in-house a few years ago, flexibility was a key requirement. 'Our focus is on getting customers to the checkout quickly and helping them find what they want,' says marketing director Mark Binnington. Boden's online arm has grown significantly and now generates 50 percent of sales in the UK and 65 percent in the US.

Such significant figures have caught the attention of many off-line retailers.

Clarks, Crew Clothing, JJB Sports and Adams Kids are a few of the retailers to have built transactional sites. When Adams Kids conducted an e-commerce trial last year, it found customers spent double what they'd typically spend in-store. Director of product Jonathan Tillery says: 'In the first year we expect to take as much as one of our largest stores.'

Despite being quick to bring grocery shopping online, the big supermarkets have been slow with clothing. Keith Chamarette, project director at digital agency WARL Evolution, which works with Tesco's clothing division, says: 'With the grocery model, someone goes round the store and puts the goods in a basket. But, the clothing department has such a high turnover of stock that it isn't mapped in the same way,' he says. 'We need to examine whether Tesco needs to move to a distribution-centre model, which is how a lot of non-food items are picked.'

But, Tesco can claim a head start on its competitors, having conducted an e-commerce pilot for some of its 'back to school' range in the summer.

Sean Murray, head of marketing for clothing marketing at Tesco, says a fully transactional site is likely to follow in the next 12 months. 'Over half the feedback we receive via e-mail asks when they can buy online,' he says.

Tesco's caution highlights retailers' fears of getting it wrong online.

'The industry is still young and there's loads of room for improvement in areas like delivery and returns,' says James Roper, chief executive of the Interactive Media in Retail Group.

But, as a lot of retailers have demonstrated, when you get it right online, the results speak for themselves in increased sales and customer loyalty, and it would be foolish for any fashion retailer to ignore this channel.

"There was a notion that luxury 'customers aren't on the Internet.'"

Some Companies Are Reluctant to Embrace Web 2.0 Technologies

Imran Amed

Imran Amed is editor of Business of Fashion, *a Web site based in the United Kingdom. In the following viewpoint, he states that some businesses in the fashion industry, particularly luxury brands, are not expanding their presence online despite the opportunities. According to Amed, established players in this market believe that Internet ventures are high-risk and luxury customers do not go online. In addition, most Web destinations for high-end shopping fail to integrate the online retail experience with interactivity and compelling content, he continues. The ones that will succeed, Amed states, will deliver both and offer unique products.*

As you read, consider the following questions:

1. How does the author support his claim that luxury customers are online?

Imran Amed, "Fashion 2.0: What the Future Holds," *The Business of Fashion* (BusinessofFashion.com), April 25, 2007. Copyright © Imran Amed 2006–2009. All rights reserved. Reproduced by permission.

2. Why are luxury brands reluctant to participate in online retail, in Imran Amed's view?

3. What has resulted from retailers' rush to the Web, according to Amed?

About a month ago [in March 2007], I attended the Harvard Business School's annual Retail and Luxury Goods Conference in Boston. It was an interesting day of speeches and panel discussions, bringing together industry veterans and experts from leading luxury goods and retail companies including Neiman Marcus, Loro Piana, and Holt Renfrew. . . .

I was honoured to speak on a panel with a diverse group of talented people from across the world of luxury goods, including the American designer Peter Som, Olivier Cardon, president of Roche Bobois North America, and Roberto Vedovotto, chairman of Lehman Brothers Global Luxury Goods practice. I thoroughly enjoyed the back and forth with my fellow panelists. We touched on many topics, but the one that seemed to provoke the most debate was regarding the role that the Internet and so-called "Web 2.0" technologies can play in the branding, marketing and commercial strategies of luxury and fashion companies.

A Time Warp

I have to say, it felt like being in a time warp. There was a notion that luxury "customers aren't on the Internet" and that the Internet "is too risky" for luxury brands. All of a sudden, I knew what it must have been like to be Natalie Massenet (of Net-a-Porter) or Ernst Malmsten (of Boo.com) back in 1999, making a case for the potential of luxury and the Internet, to people who were very risk-averse, conservative and stuck in old mind-sets; people who couldn't see the potential for what the Internet could do for their brands and businesses. Of course Boo.com and Net-a-Porter have followed two very different stories. (One, which ended abruptly, was discussed in this post.) Massenet, however, has shown (with her company that is now turning over a reported $80m [million] and growing at 100% per year), that as with all businesses, harnessing the power of the Internet for luxury comes down to basic business acumen, strong marketing skills, and knowing how to properly manage and grow a start-up, while also understanding technological issues such as the adoption curve and limitations of sophisticated technologies.

As for luxury customers not being on the Internet, this appears to be an assumption made in the absence of basic facts or data. One need only look at a recent article from the *Financial Times* to see really how many luxury customers are online:

"A survey of 500 of America's richest families published in 2005 by researchers Doug Harrison and Jim Taylor found that the respondents spent on average 13.7 hours a week online. The Luxury Institute, in a survey of 1,000 wealthy consumers published in March [2007], found that 98 percent used the Internet for shopping, and that 88 percent read product research and review sites."

Clearly, these are not just young bucks trying to pick each other up on MySpace or Facebook, but also high net worth communities like asmallworld and focused fashion communities like Iqons.com. Big brands and collections are being discussed passionately on all of these highly-trafficked sites, but also on blogs (purseblog.com, whowhatweardaily) and virtual communities (secondlife.com). The amount of content is mind-boggling.

Risk and Opportunity

Obviously not all of it is good content. But, my basic point is that since conversations about Gucci, Prada and Burberry are going on, Gucci, Prada and Burberry might as well figure out a way to be part of those discussions, where it makes sense. The fact of the matter is that the conversations will continue,

Missing the Boat on Web Strategy

Analysts expect e-commerce to account for a slightly larger chunk of retail sales in the next few years, but they say some traditionally bricks-and-mortar companies are in danger of missing the boat because they lack a sound Web strategy. "Many retailers have dropped the ball," said Larry Freed, chief executive of ForeSee Results Inc., an e-commerce research firm in Ann Arbor, Mich. "A strong online presence is no longer a luxury for retailers. It's a requirement."

David Kesmodel,
"Despite Growth of E-Commerce,
Some Retailers Remain Offline,"
The Wall Street Journal Online, *May 2, 2006.*

whether they are involved or not. Of course, not all of those places would make sense for every brand all the time, but to disregard the importance of the Internet outright seems short-sighted.

When it comes to the riskiness of luxury brands on the Internet, I can certainly appreciate this point. Big players have the most at stake, given the energy and money that have been invested in their brands, sometimes over hundreds of years. But that said, where there is risk, there is also opportunity. Thankfully, some big brands have recognised this and started to experiment with some of these new communication channels. Armani and Karl Lagerfeld have brought their fashion show videos to the Internet, iPods and mobile phones, showing that being a pioneer has nothing to do with age, it has to do with attitude. Dior has also experimented with the launch of a jewelry collection on secondlife.com.

That said, some of the most exciting ways to really experience what online luxury might feel like in the future is by visiting the amazing virtual worlds created by emerging designers, who are able take more risks and experiment. Boudicca's site at platform13.com is like walking right into the fantastical (sometimes incomprehensible) world of the designers, Zoe [Broach] and Brian [Kirby], who share all aspects of themselves and their passions. They have also uploaded all of their fashion shows to YouTube. Other fashion designers are also providing a peek into their everyday lives by keeping regularly updated blogs. New York–based Brit Sue Stemp and dynamic British-Japanese duo Eley Kishimoto are amongst those using blogs to create a space to communicate with their customers.

Fashionably Late

What the future holds for luxury e-commerce in particular is very exciting indeed, because much of the basic foundation has been laid. Competition is just beginning to heat up. Since pioneers like Massenet successfully brought luxury online, all of the big retail and luxury players have jumped in. You could say, they have been fashionably late. Neiman Marcus's direct business (which includes the nm.com, bergdorfgoodman.com and the catalogue business) now generates $700m in revenue. Revenue growth rates for the online boutiques of Coach and Gucci are massive, somewhere in the 60%+ range. Interestingly, partially because of the rush to capture online real estate and market share quickly, almost every online luxury site feels the same. Not much time has really been spent in creating a truly unique destination. Just check out brittique.com, matchesfashion.com, brownsfashion.com, neimanmarcus.com, eLuxury.com, and bluefly.com and you will see what I mean. For the most part, each site is a one-way interaction with the consumer. They also tend to be organized in the same way, with similar aesthetics using similar fonts and layout. Only

Net-a-Porter has successfully integrated compelling content into their site (with its magazine) and just Yoox has a truly different look and feel.

So now, as with any other business where the product/service starts to become commoditised, the key players will have to take it to the next level and differentiate themselves to keep up with the rapid pace of what's going on. It's not a zero sum game yet because the industry's growth is so high, but with so many players in the game, it's bound to be more competitive. This is where Web 2.0 can play a role. Luxury e-commerce sites which differentiate themselves through unique product assortments, clever editorial and content, and interactive community development, will be the ones that succeed. On the other hand, with retail it always comes down to number of visits and average purchase size, so it's also important that the interactivity and community don't detract from the primary objective at hand, which is to drive sales.

Periodical Bibliography

The following articles have been selected to supplement the diverse views presented in this chapter.

Jefferson Hack	"The Edge of Reason," *Telegraph*, May 23, 2007.
Rachel Holmes	"What's the Big Deal About Haute Couture?" *Guardian*, July 3, 2008.
Ruth La Ferla	"Uncruel Beauty," *New York Times*, January 11, 2007.
Robert Murphy	"The New Garde," *WWD*, April 9, 2007.
Christina Passariello and Stacy Meichtry	"The Couture Road Show," *Wall Street Journal*, July 7, 2007.
Nadine Rubin	"The Height of Fashion Marketing," ABC News, May 9, 2007.
Miles Socha	"Second Life: Designers Are Creating Flashback Fashion Moments with Re-Editions of Vintage Looks," *W*, April 2009.
Robert Sullivan	"Global Shopping: Extreme Seasons," *Vogue*, March 2006.
Dana Thomas	"Cloaked in Green," *Portfolio*, September 2008.
Emily Wilson	"How the Luxury Industry Went the Way of McDonald's," *Alternet*, September 19, 2007.

For Further Discussion

Chapter 1

1. Fred Schwarz states that blaming the fashion industry for eating disorders undermines the understanding of anorexia and bulimia as diseases. In your opinion, do Janet L. Treasure, Elizabeth R. Wack, and Marion E. Roberts succeed in balancing their allegations against the fashion industry with the disease model of eating disorders? Use examples from the viewpoint in your answer.

2. Do you agree with Elizabeth Bryant that plus-size models are gaining visibility in the fashion industry? Why or why not?

3. In your view, does Ryan Pintado-Vertner successfully address the issue of racism in the fashion industry? Explain your answer.

Chapter 2

1. Vivia Chen argues that counterfeiting harms luxury brands because they cut into sales. Mark Ritson, however, insists that purchases of high-end knockoffs do not cut into the sales of genuine products. In your opinion, who makes the more persuasive argument? Use examples from the viewpoints to support your response.

2. Elisabeth Rosenthal claims that fast-fashion garments are ecologically friendly because caring for them consumes less energy and water. In your opinion, does this advantage outweigh the supposed benefits of organic cotton? Explain your answer.

3. In your view, do H&M's guidelines and measures adequately protect garment workers' safety, wages, and rights? Why or why not?

Chapter 3

1. Do you agree with Julian Sanchez that copying designs in the fashion industry drives trends and innovation? Why or why not?

2. Lindsay Beyerstein maintains that weight requirements for models in Spain are arbitrary. In your opinion, do the guidelines that the Academy for Eating Disorders recommends for the fashion industry evaluate models' health and well-being on a case-by-case basis? Use examples from the viewpoints to support your answer.

Chapter 4

1. Larry Elliott declares that the tradition of haute couture is flourishing. Bridget Foley insists, however, that couture is in decline because of its high costs and the innovative contributions of ready-to-wear designers. In your opinion, who makes the more compelling argument? Explain your answer.

2. In your view, does Brita Belli convincingly address the problem of regulation in sustainable fashion? Why or why not?

3. Victoria Furness and Imran Amed both assert that fashion retail online faces usability issues. Which author presents the more practical problems, in your opinion? Use examples from the viewpoints to support your response.

Organizations to Contact

The editors have compiled the following list of organizations concerned with the issues debated in this book. The descriptions are derived from materials provided by the organizations. All have publications or information available for interested readers. The list was compiled on the date of publication of the present volume; the information provided here may change. Be aware that many organizations take several weeks or longer to respond to inquiries, so allow as much time as possible.

Academy for Eating Disorders (AED)
111 Deer Lake Road, Suite 100, Deerfield, IL   60015
(847) 498-4274 • fax: (847) 480-9282
e-mail: info@aedweb.org
Web site: www.aedweb.org

Headquartered in Illinois, the Academy for Eating Disorders (AED) is an international organization for eating disorder treatment, research, and education. It provides professional training and education, inspires new developments in eating disorders research, prevention, and clinical treatments, and is the international source for eating disorders information. The AED upholds that the beauty and fashion industries should promote a healthy body image and address eating disorders within the modeling profession.

British Fashion Council
5 Portland Place, London   W1B 1PW
   UK
+44-02076367788
e-mail: info@britishfashioncouncil.com
Web site: www.britishfashioncouncil.com

The British Fashion Council was formed in 1983 from the Fashion Industry Action Group, an ad hoc group created in 1981. The council aims to showcase British designers and develop London's position as a major player in the international fashion arena. As a result, London Fashion Week ranks alongside New York, Milan, and Paris as one of the "Big Four."

Centre for Sustainable Fashion
London College of Fashion, London   W1G 0BJ
  UK
+44-02075148470
e-mail: sustainability@fashion.arts.ac.uk
Web site: www.sustainable-fashion.com

The Centre for Sustainable Fashion at London College of Fashion connects research, education, and business to support, inspire, and create innovative approaches to fashion. It sponsors the Fashioning the Future student competition and a program that supports sustainable fashion businesses. The centre's blog offers news and information on green fashion, events, and scholarships.

Council of Fashion Designers of America (CFDA)
1412 Broadway, Suite 2006, New York, NY   10018
Web site: www.cfda.com

The Council of Fashion Designers of America (CFDA) is a not-for-profit trade association of more than three hundred of America's foremost fashion and accessory designers. Founded in 1962, the CFDA continues to advance the status of fashion design as a branch of American art and culture, to raise its artistic and professional standards, to define a code of ethical practices of mutual benefit in public and trade relations, and to promote appreciation of the fashion arts through leadership in quality and aesthetic discernment.

Fashion Group International (FGI)
8 West Fortieth Street, 7th Floor, New York, NY   10018
(212) 302-5511 • fax: (212) 302-5533
Web site: http://newyork.fgi.org

Fashion Group International (FGI) is a global, nonprofit, professional organization with five thousand members in the fashion industry including apparel, accessories, beauty, and home. The FGI provides insight on major trends in person, online, and in print; access to business professionals; and a gateway to the influence fashion plays in the marketplace. The group offers a student site, and its Fashion History Slide Archives are the largest and most comprehensive in the world.

Federal Trade Commission (FTC)

Consumer Response Center, Washington, DC 20580

(877) 382-4357 (FTC-HELP)

Web site: www.ftc.gov

The Federal Trade Commission (FTC) deals with issues that touch the economic life of every American. It is the only federal agency with both consumer protection and competition jurisdiction in broad sectors of the economy. The FTC pursues vigorous and effective law enforcement; advances consumers' interests by sharing its expertise with federal and state legislatures and U.S. and international government agencies; develops policy and research tools through hearings, workshops, and conferences; and creates educational programs for consumers and businesses in a global marketplace with constantly changing technologies.

Garment Worker Center (GWC)

1250 South Los Angeles Street, Suite 213

Los Angeles, CA 90015

(888) 449-6115

Web site: www.garmentworkercenter.org

The Garment Worker Center (GWC) is a nonprofit, membership-based organization for garment workers in California—the center of the garment industry in the United States. It provides monthly educational workshops that explain issues such as wage and hour laws, health and safety regulations, and discrimination. The center also functions as a space to centralize the efforts happening against sweatshops and help garment workers.

Sustainable Cotton Project (SCP)
PO Box 363, Davis, CA 95617
(530) 756-8518, ext. 34 • fax: (530) 756-7857
Web site: www.sustainablecotton.org

Located in California's Central Valley, the world's most productive agricultural region, Sustainable Cotton Project (SCP) focuses on the production and use of cotton, one of the most widely grown and chemical-intensive crops in the world. Since 1996, SCP has brought farmers, manufacturers, and consumers together. Its Web site offers a carbon footprint calculator for businesses and buyers.

U.S. Copyright Office
Library of Congress, Copyright Office
Washington, DC 20559-6000
(202) 707-3000
Web site: www.copyright.gov

The U.S. Copyright Office provides expert assistance to Congress on intellectual property matters, advises Congress on anticipated changes in U.S. copyright law, analyzes and assists in drafting copyright legislation and legislative reports, and provides and undertakes studies for Congress.

World Fashion Council (WFC)
24B Monroe Street, Norwalk, CT 06854
(203) 345-0030
Web site: http://worldfashioncouncil.org

The World Fashion Council (WFC) is an organization supporting young designers; encouraging innovation in design, excellence in fashion, and design education; and raising industry standards for trend, market forecasting, and consulting. WFC holds an annual international student competition called the World Fashion Council Awards, and offers various workshops and seminars.

Bibliography of Books

Karl Aspelund   *Fashioning Society: A Hundred Years of Haute Couture by Six Designers.* New York: Fairchild Publications, 2009.

Sandy Black   *Eco-Chic: The Fashion Paradox.* London: Black Dog Publishing, 2008.

Tamsin Blanchard   *Green Is the New Black: How to Change the World with Style.* New York: Williams Morrow, 2008.

Regina Lee Blaszczyk, ed.   *Producing Fashion: Commerce, Culture, and Consumers.* Philadelphia, PA: University of Pennsylvania Press, 2008.

Ethel C. Brooks   *Unraveling the Garment Industry: Transnational Organizing and Women's Work.* Minneapolis, MN: University of Minnesota Press, 2007.

Valerie Cumming   *Understanding Fashion History.* Hollywood, CA: Costume & Fashion Press, 2004.

Hywel Davies   *Modern Menswear.* London: Lawrence King Publishers, 2008.

Alicia Drake   *The Beautiful Fall: Lagerfeld, Saint Laurent, and Glorious Excess in 1970s Paris.* New York: Little, Brown and Company, 2006.

Bonnie English   *A Cultural History of Fashion in the Twentieth Century: From the Catwalk to the Sidewalk.* New York: Berg Press, 2007.

Tiffany Godoy   *Style Deficit Disorder: Harajuku Street Fashion—Tokyo.* San Francisco, CA: Chronicle Books, 2007.

Michelle M. Granger   *Fashion: The Industry and Its Careers.* New York: Fairchild Publications, 2007.

Janet Hethorn and Connie Ulasewicz   *Sustainable Fashion: Why Now? A Conversation Exploring Issues, Practices, and Possibilities.* New York: Fairchild Publications, 2008.

Yuniya Kawamura   *Fashion-ology: An Introduction to Fashion Studies.* New York: Oxford University Press, 2005.

Harold Koda   *Extreme Beauty: The Body Transformed.* New York: Metropolitan Museum of Art, 2004.

Veronica Manlow   *Designing Clothes: Culture and Organization of the Fashion Industry.* Edison, NJ: Transaction Publishers, 2009.

Peter McNeil and Vicki Karaminas, eds.   *The Men's Fashion Reader.* New York: Berg Press, 2009.

Moisés Naím   *Illicit: How Smugglers, Traffickers, and Copycats are Hijacking the Global Economy.* New York: Anchor Books, 2006.

Tim Phillips   *Knockoff: The Deadly Trade in Counterfeit Goods: The True Story of the World's Fastest Growing Crime Wave*. Philadelphia, PA: Kogan Page, 2005.

Pietra Rivoli   *The Travels of a T-Shirt in the Global Economy: An Economist Examines the Markets, Power, and Politics of World Trade*. Hoboken, NJ: John Wiley & Sons, 2009.

Valerie Steele and Jennifer Park   *Gothic: Dark Glamour*. New Haven, CT: Yale University Press, 2008.

Radu Stern   *Against Fashion: Clothing as Art, 1850–1930*. Cambridge, MA: MIT Press, 2004.

Style.com, ed.   *Stylist: The Interpreters of Fashion*. New York: Rizzoli, 2007.

Lars Svendsen   *Fashion: A Philosophy*. London: Reaktion Books, 2006.

Sharon S. Takeda and Kaye D. Spilker   *Breaking the Mode*. New York: Skira, 2007.

Dana Thomas   *Deluxe: How Luxury Lost Its Luster*. New York: Penguin Press, 2007.

Mark Tungate   *Fashion Brands: Branding Style from Armani to Zara*. Philadelphia, PA: Kogan Page, 2008.

Steven Vogel   *Streetwear: The Insider's Guide*. San Francisco, CA: Chronicle Books, 2007.

Index